160901

Gil G. Noam
Editor-in-Chief

NEW DIRECTIONS FOR YOUTH DEVELOPMENT

Theory
Practice
Research

winter | 2005

Doing the Right Thing

Ethical Development Across Diverse Environments

issue
Dale Borman Fink | *editor*

This issue is a collaboration between *New Directions for Youth Development* and the National AfterSchool Association.

JOSSEY-BASS™
An Imprint of
⊛WILEY

Doing the Right Thing: Ethical Development Across Diverse Environments
Dale Borman Fink (ed.)
New Directions for Youth Development, No. 108, Winter 2005
Gil G. Noam, Editor-in-Chief

Microfilm copies of issues and articles are available in 16mm and 35mm, as well as microfiche in 105mm, through University Microfilms Inc., 300 North Zeeb Road, Ann Arbor, Michigan 48106-1346.

New Directions for Youth Development (ISSN 1533-8916, electronic ISSN 1537-5781) is part of The Jossey-Bass Psychology Series and is published quarterly by Wiley Subscription Services, Inc., A Wiley Company, at Jossey-Bass, 989 Market Street, San Francisco, California 94103-1741. POSTMASTER: Send address changes to New Directions for Youth Development, Jossey-Bass, 989 Market Street, San Francisco, California 94103-1741.

Subscriptions cost $80.00 for individuals and $180.00 for institutions, agencies, and libraries. Prices subject to change. Refer to the order form at the back of this issue.

Editorial correspondence should be sent to the Editor-in-Chief, Dr. Gil G. Noam, McLean Hospital, 115 Mill Street, Belmont, MA 02478.

Cover photograph by sw productions © Picture Quest

www.josseybass.com

Contents

Editor-in-Chief's Notes

Dear Readers,

NEW DIRECTIONS for Youth Development is now in its fourth year. This is our 12th issue and we have very exciting new ones planned. When we began, there was a great deal of skepticism about how viable a journal would be in the field of youth development. We were told it was not really a field, that people in this non-existing field neither read nor write, and that research, policy, and practice do not meaningfully inform each other. The closing of a number of publications supported this perspective. Fortunately, not everyone was a pessimist. In fact, many people we talked to were very excited and saw the need for an in-depth topical journal. But the worry about fragmentation and lack of intellectual coherence was great enough that few publishers dared to pursue a new publication initiative. But Jossey-Bass, an imprint of Wiley, with their large journal offerings in related fields and their Internet presence, joined with us to build a journal that could succeed.

It was clear that to achieve this goal we would have to address topics of relevance to the field, from changing educational practices to the growing afterschool movement, to critiques of punitive practices through zero tolerance and prison pipelines, to trauma, mentoring, and youth worker training. We also wanted to expand the contributors and to create a forum for a vibrant group of theorists, researchers, and policy-makers. We further wanted to present an opportunity for practitioners to convey the amazing creativity in the field. We want the boundary between readers and authors to be a fluid one. Authors read and readers can write, and that includes youth! So far, over one hundred authors have written pieces, and

NEW DIRECTIONS FOR YOUTH DEVELOPMENT, NO. 108, WINTER 2005 © WILEY PERIODICALS, INC.

each issue continues to expand the group of authors. And from what we can tell, the Journal is receiving increasing numbers of unsolicited proposals for issues and articles. The growing correspondence also indicates that readers are engaged and want more.

And more is needed. We want to be the preeminent journal and intellectual source for the youth development field. We want to reach the multiple audiences of youth workers and program leaders, scholars and rabble-rousers, policy-makers and funders. We want to contribute to an intense and needed dialogue between school leaders and teachers and youth development practitioners, between mental health and health professionals and community organizers, between politicians and academics and families. This is the exciting part of all of our work: it does not belong to any one party or group, one organization or institution. Instead it exists in-between and across boundaries—something I have termed in this journal the "intermediary spaces" of innovation, scholarship, and practice.

To reach the potential of interdisciplinary dialogue on a large scale, we have taken a very exciting step: Judy Nee, the president of the National AfterSchool Association (NAA), and I are excited to announce a partnership between the Journal and the NAA (previously NSACA—National School Age Care Alliance), an 8,500-member organization with a visionary president, a great managing director, Peter Howe, and a very accomplished publication committee headed by Selma Goore. We will jointly publish one issue per year on a specific topic. This issue is the first fruit of our joint labor.

Dale Fink, an active member of the publications committee of NAA, served as the editor of this issue. The topic of ethical development is a critical one. While a great deal has been published on character development and moral education in schools, very little writing has occurred for the out-of-school field. Afterschool and summer experiences are typically viewed as ideal settings to increase social skills, interpersonal empathy, and civic engagement. But this reality has not led to systematic thinking about the role of setting in enhancing this essential strand of development. This joint issue between NDYD and NAA is an example of how we can insure the growth of a topic that has direct implications on how we work with young people. Dale accomplished this task in record time and with excellent editorial judgment and care.

We look forward to a long working relationship with the NAA, and will ensure that the annual issue will be ready for the NAA conference held each February. We will name two members of NAA who are contributors in their fields to join the editorial board. David Famiano, an editor of journals at Jossey-Bass who has a special interest in youth development, has been flexible and supportive in making this and other arrangements possible.

To continue to assure not only inclusion but also highest quality, we have decided that the Journal will become more fully peer reviewed in 2006. We are lucky to have the best advisory board one can hope for, and the board members as well as many other contributors to the field will determine the quality of issues and help us to support writers in producing the best work possible.

One more change is occurring: We are receiving a growing number of manuscripts that are not topically linked to a specific issue in preparation. For that reason we will also publish issues that will highlight the best papers that have undergone a rigorous peer review. This way we can support the careers of young investigators who up to now have had a difficult time publishing their work on specific topics of youth development, and youth development influenced education, health, and mental health. There also has not been a peer-reviewed journal that has developed scholarly criteria for publishing programs and innovations and exciting new practices and case studies in youth development. We are currently accepting papers for the first non-topical issue of *New Directions in Youth Development*, and you are welcome to send yours to us.

We feel lucky that we can make all of these additions to our journal without losing the very special aspect of our work: that each issue is also sold separately, available in bookstores and from Amazon.com and many other sources. I strongly believe in bringing together authors that have a wide array of knowledge to address a single topic in depth. I find it very exciting when a program director and funder read one of our issues to get support for their ideas when they write a grant or fund a project. Or when a program is in touch with another program because they heard about a new practice through an article in our Journal. We want more policy-makers to use the insights developed in these issues and for that reason we created the executive summaries. But it is not easy to cross all of these boundaries. For that we need all of us to work together, and the Journal is a vehicle enabling us to do so. I am sure we can continue to help in this significant work of creating momentum for an intellectual and practical movement to support youth by building on their strengths, abilities, and ingenuity without losing sight of the challenges and risks for them and for the hundreds of thousands of people who dedicate their careers to their well-being.

Sincerely,

Gil G. Noam
Editor-in-Chief

P.S.: To stay in touch with new developments of the Journal and to get information about future issues and information for authors and editors, go to Pearweb.org (PEAR stands for Program in Education, Afterschool and Resilience, an initiative of Harvard University and McLean Hospital in collaboration with a variety of community health, education, and youth-serving organizations).

Issue Editor's Notes

WE COMPLETED THE editorial work on this issue while citizens and political leaders in the United States reflected on the suffering and death that transpired recently on our Gulf coast. What went wrong in the preparation for and response to Hurricane Katrina? Questions of ethics made their way into the discussions. Did individuals living in poverty receive a less emphatic federal response than would have been offered to more affluent citizens facing a similar natural disaster? Whose choices led to the environmental neglect that intensified the storm's destructive power?

The post-Katrina discussion is only one recent example of how important a well-developed sense of ethics is to being a full participant in our society. Yet for those of us involved in guiding young people toward mature decision making in the arena of ethics, it is frustrating how frequently we encounter unscrupulous characters who have become leaders of business, education, politics, or other fields. Some of our most prominent felons (think Enron, Tyco, WorldCom) were only recently celebrated as entrepreneurial geniuses. On top of that, youth ethics sometimes gets reduced to calls for better behavior, by which is meant *compliance*: follow the rules, avoid drugs and sex, respect authority. But I have never seen any evidence that more compliant (or more drug-free or more sexually abstinent) individuals make more ethically sound decisions. Moral exemplars such as Gandhi, Martin Luther King Jr., and Nelson Mandela have taught us that persons imbued with a strong sense of ethics will not only challenge authority themselves but will motivate their peers to do the same.

If the adult leaders in our society do not consistently exemplify ethical values and actions, then it is all the more pressing that those

NEW DIRECTIONS FOR YOUTH DEVELOPMENT, NO. 108, WINTER 2005 © WILEY PERIODICALS, INC.

involved with youth pay attention to this domain. We do not have the luxury of designing an ethical world first and then helping young people fit into it. Instead, we must assist them in recognizing that there are right and wrong ways to act and to treat others—even if they perceive, accurately, that the relationship in our society between ethical decision making and tangible success is tenuous at best. In putting out a call for chapters, we hoped to learn that operators of some out-of-school programs had found a way to add guidance on ethics to the long list of priorities they were already juggling—helping children with homework, expanding cultural horizons, facilitating conflict resolution with peers, and attending to basic needs such as snacks, vigorous physical exercise, and fresh air. We hoped, too, to find some scholars or practitioners who have gathered data regarding the ethical understandings of the youth they serve or even designed interventions to influence those understandings.

The response exceeded our hopes. We received thought-provoking submissions from a multiplicity of scholars and program operators. The social milieus our authors wrote about were wide ranging: students involved with livestock; political activists; members of an urban recreation center; sports competitors; and teenagers who spend many hours online. The submissions that we chose to publish offered important insights into how youths think about ethics or an idea for some kind of an intervention, or both.

The authors who add primarily on the insight side of the ledger are Ben Kirshner (Chapter Two), Karen Bradley (Chapter Four), Dale Fink (Chapter Five), Nancy Deutsch (Chapter Six), and Donna Peterson, James Roebuck, Sherry Betts, and Marta Stuart (Chapter Ten). Kirshner examined mostly secondary sources to consider what we can learn about moral development from the experiences of youth activists. Bradley built on interviews, correspondence, and discussions with adolescents who were active online, as well as secondary sources to relate the development of ethics in cyberspace to broader understandings of ethics. Fink and Deutsch each drew from qualitative observations in such local venues as small-town Brownie troops and urban Boys and Girls

Clubs. Fink's aim was to understand the way typically developing children think about disabilities and arrive at an ethical approach to communicating with them about peers who have disabilities. Deutsch used her extended engagement with a small number of youngsters to learn about their social and ethical values and the way a recreation center contributed to them. Peterson, Roebuck, Betts, and Stuart carried out a communitywide written survey of youth in order to find out how they thought about right and wrong and whether their actions were true to their own beliefs. Their chapter ends just at the point when they are ready to cross the bridge from insight to intervention.

The chapters that fall more strongly on the intervention side of the ledger are by Clinton Rusk, Keli Brubaker, Mark Balschweid, and Edmond Pajor (Chapter Three), Elizabeth Devaney, Mary O'Brien, Mary Tavegia, and Hank Resnik (Chapter Seven), Ginny Deerin (Chapter Eight), and Kathleen Lodl (Chapter Nine). Rusk, Brubaker, Balschweid, and Pajor introduced an ethics curriculum to high school agriculture students and evaluated its impact by way of a test and retest. The authors of Chapters Seven and Eight are devotees of social and emotional learning (SEL), and both chapters begin from the insight that learning is a social and emotional process. Qualitative descriptions of activities and outcomes are the primary data they share. Devaney, O'Brien, Tavegia, and Resnik introduce the overall SEL rationale and then take readers inside one public school that has implemented it. Deerin uses a zoom lens, inviting us to see up close the kinds of responses to youth with challenging behaviors that characterize the program she founded. Lodl shares what must be the most ambitious intervention discussed in this issue: an attempt to engage entire communities in injecting more ethics into sports and other competitive arenas, enlisting adult coaches and fans along with youthful competitors and their peers.

Chapter One, by Joyce Walker, Cecilia Gran, and Arnoldo Curiel, does not fit neatly into either of these lists. The authors put forth approximately equal parts insight and ideas for interventions. Their insights are drawn not from formal research but from informal observations over the course of their work. They have also not tested the interventions they recommend through formal inquiry. Nevertheless, this is important to publish because it addresses in a meaningful way a key question: How can youth workers become skilled and practiced at placing their own actions within an ethical framework?

In Chapters One and Nine, ethics are viewed explicitly as something much more than a "youth problem." Both target the education of adults as central to any effort to guide young men and women in an ethical direction. In several other chapters, the same message is implicit. This may finally be the most important lesson from this issue of *New Directions for Youth Development*. It is feasible for adults to pass along reading and study skills, dance steps, recipes, scientific concepts, and jump-shooting techniques to the young. In high-quality out-of-school programs and activities, such transfer of knowledge from the more experienced to the less experienced takes place every day. But in the arena of ethics, it would be a mistake to assume that more experienced equals more ethically developed. Sometimes the adults are in need of guidance. And sometimes the young can be our teachers.

Dale Borman Fink
Editor

DALE BORMAN FINK *is an independent scholar based in Williamstown, Massachusetts. He also holds a faculty appointment at the University of Connecticut Center for Excellence in Developmental Disabilities.*

Executive Summary

Prologue: Mechanical Man

Astrid Liden

We lead off this issue of the journal with a poem crafted by an eleven-year-old girl. It offers us one preadolescent's emerging understanding about how the rhythms and obligations of life in a modern society can sometimes overwhelm the capacity of adults to perceive and express deeper truths, including ethical concerns.

Chapter One: Shaping ethics: Youth workers matter

Joyce A. Walker, Cecilia F. Gran, Arnoldo Curiel

The authors propose that youth workers and educators committed to informing and shaping the ethical understandings of young people first need to explore and become aware of their own ethics. This requires front-line staff and caregivers to critically reflect on the impact their day-to-day choices and decisions have on youth. Once they become clearer about their own ethics and the consequences of their decisions, youth workers are then in a position to promote opportunities for youth to make ethical choices. The authors use observations and ideas from their experiences with the Minnesota Youth Work Institute. Their overarching aim is to promote ethical congruence between what is taught, how it is taught, and how it is practiced in daily work with youth.

NEW DIRECTIONS FOR YOUTH DEVELOPMENT, NO. 108, WINTER 2005 © WILEY PERIODICALS, INC.

Chapter Two: Moral voices of politically engaged urban youth

Ben Kirshner

The relationship between reflection and action is an enduring question for those interested in promoting moral development among young people. Educators struggle to find effective methods for helping youth reason carefully about moral problems and also to show moral commitment in their everyday lives. One place where reflection and action come together is in youth activism, where young people engage in social action campaigns to improve their schools and communities. What are the moral concerns that urban youth raise when given the opportunity? How do these concerns get translated into action? Drawing on original and secondary sources, this chapter discusses four social action campaigns organized by youth in the San Francisco Bay Area, in which youth combined critical moral judgments with social action. The chapter is not an empirical study, but instead an effort to bring attention to the moral and ethical perspectives that politically engaged youth raise. These social action projects suggest that for youth living in low-income neighborhoods with limited resources, the capacity for critical moral reflection about one's surroundings is an important dimension of healthy development. Helping youth assess and transform their local environments represents a promising direction for moral education and youth development.

Chapter Three: Capitalizing on the human-animal bond to teach ethics to youth

Clinton P. Rusk, Keli M. Brubaker, Mark A. Balschweid, Edmond A. Pajor

The purpose of this study was to evaluate the effectiveness of a livestock ethics curriculum developed for high school students in agricultural education classes. The curriculum was developed in response to numerous unethical occurrences at major livestock shows in recent years. These have included drug violations, physical alteration of animals, and excessive involvement of professional livestock handlers. The curriculum was taught to 305 students enrolled in eight Indiana high school agriculture programs. Data were collected using a pretest and posttest. Eighty-six percent of participants improved their score from the pretest to the posttest. Participants increased their awareness and knowledge of the overall principles involved in making ethical choices when faced with decisions in youth livestock programs. Students improved their understanding of the consequences associated with making unethical choices when faced with decisions in the youth livestock program. Participants were more likely to make an ethical choice when faced with a scenario featuring an ethical dilemma. Participants who had previously been enrolled in 4-H, Future Farmers of America, or an animal project had higher scores than those who had not been previously enrolled, but the amount of change from pre- to posttest was similar for those with and without such prior exposure. Future research should examine whether mastery of this kind of ethics curriculum will lead to better ethical choices in real-life situations.

Chapter Four: Internet lives: Social context and moral domain in adolescent development

Karen Bradley

The author examines the thinking and behavior of adolescents within the digital world. What does all this instant messaging and blogging outside school hours mean? Why do adolescents do it? How much time do they spend doing it? How does it shape their social, emotional, and moral development? Bradley describes the phenomenon and explores some moral development ramifications of a new context of social experience for adolescents. It proposes that the digital world creates its own social context, with a different set of social conventions from the adult-mediated "real" world that adolescents also inhabit. It is a social context that most adults are aware of but do not understand. Adolescents' experiences in the online world influence their experiences in the face-to-face world and play an important role in the development of their social and moral knowledge. This chapter places the discussion within the context of literature on youth ethics that has been developed based on more traditional settings.

Chapter Five: Toward ethical approaches to the inclusion of peers with disabilities

Dale Borman Fink

What would it mean for program leaders and caregivers to shape the thinking of typically developing youth toward their peers with disabilities in a way that we could regard as ethically sound? The author weaves examples from his research in settings such as Girl Scout troops and Boys and Girls Clubs as well as his own parenting experiences to answer this question. He has found that it is commonplace for program leaders, coaches, and others to avoid direct discussion or acknowledgment of the disabilities of children in their groups, in the mistaken belief that this is the best way to demonstrate that all children are equal and to avoid the perception of discrimination. His interpretation is that this is not a product of thoughtlessness but of caring staff and volunteers who believe they are doing the right thing—the ethical thing—by avoiding acknowledgment of individual differences. Disabilities—even when they are readily apparent—are treated as if they were invisible. Rather than giving disabilities the "silent treatment," the author challenges us to go beyond the prevailing ethos and find ways to build on naturally occurring opportunities to learn more about individual needs and supports.

Chapter Six: "I like to treat others as others would treat me": The development of prosocial selves in an urban youth organization

Nancy L. Deutsch

The development of moral identity is linked to a sense of self that is prosocial and connected to others. Youth organizations, if designed appropriately, may provide a setting for social interactions and relationships in which youth can enact and receive validation for moral behaviors and develop prosocial selves. This chapter reports on findings from a four-year study of identity construction within an urban Boys and Girls Club. The author conducted interviews and photography projects with seventeen youth ages twelve to eighteen, all of whom were active club members. Over half described their race or ethnicity as black or African American, while others were Hispanic, Afro-Latino, white, or other. All of them either lived in the housing project near the club or had close ties to it. Both boys and girls describe themselves as rooted in a rich relational milieu that promoted prosocial identities. The importance of respect emerged as a key theme in the teens' narratives about themselves and their activities. The author found that the club served as a site for the development of prosocial traits in an environment characterized by respectful and supportive relationships.

Chapter Seven: Promoting children's ethical development through social and emotional learning

Elizabeth Devaney, Mary Utne O'Brien, Mary Tavegia, Hank Resnik

In today's climate of increased emphasis on measuring achievement through high-stakes testing, academic subjects are too often divorced from the social context in which they are taught. We know that learning is a social process. In fact, many educators and other youth development practitioners recognize that social, emotional, and ethical development cannot be ignored in the name of better academic preparation, especially in the face of data showing that students are more disengaged than ever before. Social and emotional learning (SEL) offers educators and other youth development personnel a framework for addressing students' social and emotional needs in systematic way. SEL is the process of acquiring the skills to recognize and manage emotions, develop caring and concern for others, establish positive relationships, make responsible decisions, and handle challenging situations effectively. Research has shown that SEL has an impact on every aspect of children's development: their health, ethical development, citizenship, academic learning, and motivation to achieve. This chapter profiles one school in Illinois that has been implementing SEL programming for a number of years. The authors provide evidence of the impact of SEL on school climate, student behavior, and attitudes. Ultimately the authors see this as fostering the kind of understanding of the larger world that leads young people to make ethical choices. They propose that the lessons learned are applicable to a wide variety of settings, including other schools, after-school programs, and summer camps.

Chapter Eight: Giving youth the social and emotional skills to succeed

Ginny Deerin

WINGS for Kids is a nonprofit organization based in Charleston, South Carolina, that aims to supply the social and emotional learning (SEL) component into existing programs for school-aged children and thereby assist them to recognize and manage emotions, care about others, make good decisions, behave ethically and responsibly, build satisfying relationships, and avoid negative behaviors. The author, who is the founder and CEO of WINGS, traces the ethos of the organization to her own life experiences as well as her observations of low-income children and families more generally. She describes the strategies and practices that character- ize the WINGS approach to SEL. The chapter focuses on the progress made by one boy, who arrived at WINGS at the age of seven, got into disputes from the very first day, and was eventually ejected from the WINGS program but later earned his way back with a commitment to change. He sustained his involvement for a number of years and became an exemplar of what the author states they are trying to accomplish.

Chapter Nine: Developing a game plan for good sportsmanship

Kathleen Lodl

It is widely believed in the United States that competition is ben- eficial for youngsters. However, the media are full of examples of players, fans, and coaches whose behavior veers out of control. There have been well-documented examples of youth in livestock competitions illegally medicating show animals to make them appear calmer, officials biasing their rulings toward a team that will take the most fans to a playoff game, and team rivalries that have become so caustic as to be dangerous for competitors and fans. A university extension and its partners created a program called "Great Fans. Great Sports." in order to teach the kinds of behav- iors we wish to instill among all who are involved in competitions. It requires entire communities to develop and implement plans for enhancing sportsmanship in music, debate, drama, 4-H, and other arenas, as well as sports. The goal is to make good sportsmanship not the exception but the norm. The authors provide anecdotal evidence that "Great Fans. Great Sports." is having a positive impact on the attitudes and behaviors of competitors, fans, and communities.

Chapter Ten: Pathways of influence in out-of-school time: A community-university partnership to develop ethics

Donna J. Peterson, James C. Roebuck, Sherry C. Betts, Marta E. Stuart

If we wish to incorporate parents and community members as full partners in building character among youth, then the activities and programs in which youth participate during their out-of-school time are potentially important venues. This chapter describes how numerous agencies in a single community partnered with a university, with the help of the cooperative extension agent, to collect local data on how adolescents used out-of-school time, what they thought about right and wrong, and how well their own behavior comported with their understandings of what was right. Results indicated that surveyed youth characterized themselves as thinking more than acting in ethical ways. For instance, nearly half acknowledged having cheated on a test at least once in the past six months, although the vast majority thought that cheating was wrong. The three pathways the community identified for reaching youth were (1) extracurricular activities at school such as sports, yearbook, and pep club; (2) organized nonschool pursuits such as music, dance, hiking, and biking; and (3) religious activities. They found that nearly 90 percent of high school–aged respondents participated in one or another of these venues.

Prologue

Mechanical Man

Astrid Liden

On a city street, many faces.
Different, but all alike.
They stare straight ahead, in a daze,
Too busy to notice others around them.
Only thinking about themselves,
Where they are going, what they will do there.
They swarm like ants through the city,
Rushing to their jobs.
They are wind-up toys.
Winding themselves in the morning,
As the day goes on, they start to wear down.
But they keep going, tiring themselves.
Still unaware of the meaning of life,
Until finally they must stop, rest for the night.
But morning comes, again, there they are, winding.
Thinking about the day ahead.
One tries to remember the speech he will give,
Another thinks about her raise.
But they aren't thinking about the people in their lives,
Or the special little things that will make up their day.
It seems that many people are frozen in ice,
Have numbed themselves to the intangibles of life. . . .
                    BEAUTY, TRUTH, LOVE.

ASTRID LIDEN *wrote this poem when she was eleven years old, living in Pittsburgh, Pennsylvania. She is now in her thirties, working in adult literacy and English as a Second Language.*

NEW DIRECTIONS FOR YOUTH DEVELOPMENT, NO. 108, WINTER 2005 © WILEY PERIODICALS, INC.

The authors propose that if we expose youth workers to practice scenarios requiring ethical decision making, they can learn ways of intentionally and authentically modeling and transmitting ethical values to youth.

1

Shaping ethics: Youth workers matter

Joyce A. Walker, Cecilia F. Gran, Arnoldo Curiel

HAVE YOU EVER been awake at night wondering if something you did or said to a young person was professionally ethical? Do you ever find yourself thinking, "Just do as I say, not as I do," when a young person calls you on an inconsistency between your actions and your words? If so, you realize that the daily problem solving and decision making of youth workers and community-based educators in youth development programs creates a dynamic context for exploring ethics in action. As practitioners and scholars working at a university-based training institute, we believe that adults working in youth development programs and helping youth gain an ethical understanding of the world must themselves adopt some principles of ethical practice and use them to practice three habits in their professional work: personal ethical awareness, critical reflection on practice, and intentional actions in relationships and daily work with young people.

In this chapter, we explore the topic of ethics and lay out a three-step progression for integrating ethical thinking and action into daily work with young people.

NEW DIRECTIONS FOR YOUTH DEVELOPMENT, NO. 108, WINTER 2005 © WILEY PERIODICALS, INC.

Youth development work involves ethics

Through words and actions, youth workers and educators model and transmit ethical values to youth all of the time. Young people are shaping their understanding of good conduct and ethical behavior, or not, based on what they hear us say and see us do every day. We often represent what we do as right, just, and fair without much personal examination of the issues. It is easy (but misleading) to assume that our personal standards of right or good conduct are shared and that others interpret our actions and decisions to be ethical. However, since nothing we do or say is neutral, we are routinely sending messages about our ethical understandings without ever mentioning values education or the study of ethics. Therefore, it is important that youth workers and educators in youth development programs engage in personal reflection and educational experiences to sharpen their understanding and action skills related to ethical practice.

Because few youth workers and community-based educators have a chance to receive a quality education in youth development prior to entering the field, individual professional development or organizational staff development on the topic of ethics in youth work practice is important. Youth work practitioners need to understand the concept of ethical behavior as going beyond the issues of stealing, lying, cheating, or mistreating others.

One of the most important aspects of good youth development work is the ability to articulate how and why we make certain choices and decisions in our relationships with young people. So often we make decisions based on unexamined gut instincts or intuition without thinking and clearly articulating a rationale for our decisions and actions to youth. We leave it up to chance that youth will correctly interpret our decisions and actions as being fair and equitable for all. Without meaning to, we model unexamined behavior that does not make sense to others, and we lose opportunities to guide youth in shaping their understanding of ethical behavior. A good example of unexamined practice and its effects on youth follows. We call it "The Speak English Story":

In a training session, a youth worker described her challenge to handle conflicts and intervene in arguments between nonnative English-speaking and English-speaking youth at the neighborhood park and recreation center. Most of the nonnative English speakers were Hmong; the English speakers were Caucasian. She decided to require all the youth to speak English. Her rationale was that when the Hmong youth were speaking their native language, the "white" youth concluded negative things were being said about them. This understanding, she felt, caused problems to escalate. Her stated rationale was that this was America, and in America you have to speak English, so it was "fair" for her to require all the young people to speak English while at the park.

This story illustrates many dimensions of ethics in practice. What is the problem here? To what extent may you dictate the language a person uses if you feel it is a problem for others? What rules govern the decision to interfere? Would you require adults to do the same in a similar situation? What other options did the youth worker have? How might the non-English-speaking youth have interpreted this decision? And the English speakers? Why choose this solution over other possible solutions? What would you have done in this youth worker's position?

Defining ethics

While Banks and Nohr use the terms *ethics* and *morals* interchangeably, in this chapter we use *ethics* to describe the principles, norms, and standards of behavior people use to determine what is good or bad, right or wrong in their interactions with other people.[1] A simplified distinction between principle-based ethics and virtue-based ethics is useful:

- Principle-based ethics weigh right or wrong actions based on respect for individual persons[2] and personal choices, as well as on conceptions of the public good, the collective welfare, and social justice.[3]
- Virtue-based ethics weigh good and bad actions based on character traits like honesty and integrity[4] and relationship motives like caring.[5]

In practical terms, principle-based ethics ask, "Is it better to make this decision based on respecting individual differences or on promoting the common good of the group?" Virtue-based ethics ask, "What would an honest person do in this situation? How does a responsible youth worker solve this problem?" Both ethical stances are relevant to the practice ethics of youth workers and community-based educators since one speaks to principles guiding work-related decisions and actions, and the other speaks to the character traits of the adult leader that contribute to successful youth development work.

Practice ethics is a term we use to refer to the application of ethical standards to problem solving and decision making in the course of youth development work. Practice ethics are situationally located and require us to consider the individual people involved, as well as factors like race, ethnicity, culture, and community norms. Practice ethics focus on dealing with immediate, close-up issues rather than debating how to solve the grave issues of the society; nonetheless, practice ethics are tied to the traditional philosophical debates about right conduct and right action.

As educators in the youth development arena, we have concerns about respect for individual rights versus concern for the public good. We also have issues with our role and goal as educators: When do we work to empower youth, and when do we work to control youth? Adult leaders in youth development programs are continually balancing and rebalancing their relationships with the young people they work with through the conduct they encourage and the control they exert. Their leadership stance is conveyed through intentional and unintentional actions, the values they consistently apply, the conduct they expect, the achievements they reward, and the power they exert or share. Yet youth program staff receive little help in thinking about the powerful role they play in creating educational contexts and program environments where the ethical development of young people is promoted, practiced, and expected.

In the next section, we propose some principles of practice that can be used as both standards for professional conduct in the youth development workplace and as principles for individual ethical decision making. The aim is congruence in what is done, practiced, and observed in daily experience and what is explicitly taught to young people.

Adopting principles to guide ethical practice

In the absence of field-endorsed professional standards and codes of conduct for youth workers and community-based educators,[6] the Minnesota Youth Work Institute uses two principles as the basis for discussions on the values underlying program intentionality and ethical decision making in youth work practice. The first is what we call the *ethos of positive youth development*, which describes and reflects a fundamental commitment to how one acts toward and works with young people.[7] The ethos delineates six elements of intentional practice that can be used to guide relationships and ways of working in youth development settings:

1. Choice and flexibility: Choice and flexibility provide important ways for young people to have a voice in their learning and development.
2. Co-Creation: Learning and development are enhanced when young people are engaged in active co-creation with adults and other youth.
3. Grounded in everyday life: Young people benefit when opportunities for development and learning are grounded in their everyday lives.
4. Comprehensive: Young people benefit when their learning opportunities are conceived as a cohesive whole rather than constructed out of a series of fragmented events and activities.
5. Asset based: Young people benefit when structured supports and opportunities are guided by an asset-based approach.
6. Address basic youth needs: Young people benefit when programs they are engaged in address their needs.

The second principle is nested in the ethos in the sixth element and centers on the idea that all youth development programs should be intentionally structured to meet basic youth needs. The ethos can be used in youth programs to identify outcomes, clarify program strategies, and understand youth motives. Using the two sets of principles as guides, adults can gauge their ethical stance, create options, and decide on ethical action.

Konopka identified eight basic needs as requirements for healthy development of young people.[8] Youth need to:

- Feel a sense of safety and structure and experience membership and belonging
- Develop self-worth through meaningful contribution
- Have opportunities to experiment to discover themselves, gain independence, and gain control over their lives
- Develop significant positive relationships with peers and at least one adult
- Have opportunities to discuss conflicting values and form their own
- Feel pride of competence and mastery in what they do
- Have opportunities to expand their capacity to enjoy life
- Know that success is possible

The idea of an ethos of positive youth development springs from reflecting on and synthesizing our core values around working with youth. Instead of working to control behavior, prevent problems, and "fix" young people, youth workers who possess a positive youth development ethos intentionally work to meet the basic needs of youth. These adults understand that their ethical stances are taught through the programs they structure and the opportunities they create for youth. Implicit in this positive youth development ethos is the ability to establish caring and nurturing relationships with youth, find ways to engage youth where they are, have high expectations of all the youth they work with, understand the importance of continuity of their presence over time, and create opportunities for youth to contribute authentically as equal partners.

Three steps in developing and articulating practice ethics

Educational and staff development efforts to strengthen the ethical understandings of adult program leaders depend on personal ethical awareness followed by critical reflection and intentional action, not on finding a single, right ethical answer. Adults must become personally aware of and take time to examine their own ethical stances before they can expect youth to do so.[9] Youth workers and educators must also recognize and understand that their interactions with youth have ethical dimensions to them. We acknowledge that thoughtful consideration and critical examination of personal beliefs and practice are not always easy and that it can be risky to question our basic assumptions and personal philosophy around our work with youth.

This self-examination and personal awareness of the disconnection between our words and actions is made even more difficult when we recognize that this sort of critical examination cannot be a one-time event. Once we become aware of the incongruence, we must renew our commitment to do our inner homework every day and in every circumstance. It then truly does become an active ethos guiding the daily practice of our work with young people.

As you read "The Pocket Knife Story," which follows, think about the principles in the ethos of positive youth development and your ethical stand in this dilemma:

The street outreach worker worked from late evening until early morning at a shelter for homeless and runaway youth. When coworkers brought a young man off the streets to stay for the night, the worker did the standard intake, explaining the rules the youth must follow if he was to stay in the shelter. While checking him in, the worker confiscated a pocket knife. The three-inch blade was a legal item available for purchase in the camping section of any store. It was not unusual for youth living on the streets to carry weapons for protection as they made their travels. When the worker took the knife from the young man, a feeling of uneasiness rushed over him. The worker had a sense that something was not right. However, there were no external cues from the young man to warrant this feeling. The young man stayed in the shelter for several weeks. He was always engaging and compliant. As the young man went out each day, the worker gave him his belongings, including his knife. The staff debated among themselves whether he should get his knife back. The worker always advocated that he should be allowed to take his knife even though that sense of uneasiness remained. He explained that the weapon was not illegal, and confiscating it for no reason could compromise the relationship he was building with this young man.

Personal ethical awareness

Personal ethical awareness is the first step in developing a positive youth development ethos. Through exploration of personal values, adults learn to question what was formerly unquestionable and begin to see ethical issues they must deal with in their work context. They must also learn to distinguish when the issue they face poses an ethical dilemma. What was the real problem in "The Speak English Story": the failure of the youth worker to speak Hmong, the discomfort of the only-English speakers, or the lack of constructive ways to resolve conflicts? Once the problems are identified and prioritized, one can work on the solution. In terms of "The Pocket Knife Story" and personal ethical awareness, consider the following:

• What are the ethical aspects of this dilemma?
• What are your feelings about homeless youth?
• Does the responsibility for homeless youth belong primarily with the young person, the family, or society?
• Under what circumstances is it acceptable to carry a weapon around in daily life?
• What would you do in this situation if you were the street worker?

In order to guide youth workers in increasing their personal awareness of values and ethics, Banks and Nohr recommend using group analysis of video situations and sharing insights from their written learning journals as two methods to strengthen personal ethical awareness.[10] We have had success with group discussions of films like *Stand and Deliver* where a dedicated teacher tries all sorts of strategies to encourage his urban Hispanic students to pass the college Advanced Placement tests in higher mathematics.

Critical reflection on practice

Critical reflection on practice, the second step, enables youth workers to take a conscious step back to interpret, process, and synthesize what they have learned from a situation or an encounter. This kind of reflection, once learned and consistently practiced, can sharpen reasoning skills and help youth workers deal effectively with situations that are challenging, problematic, and ambiguous.[11] Young people also need to be given opportunities to sharpen critical reflection skills in order to enhance and shape their understanding of ethics.

A good example of critical reflection in practice is illustrated in the street worker's recurring concerns in "The Pocket Knife Story." In terms of critical reflection on practice:

- What basic needs is the young man seeking to fulfill?
- What do you think the young man is doing well? Poorly?
- How is the street worker honoring individual rights?
- What is the street worker's obligation to the larger community?

Philippart describes his experience in the Netherlands using Socratic dialogue as a method of practical reasoning to help youth workers discern the ethical issues of their work.[12] Similar to Kohlberg's moral dilemma scenarios,[13] this method uses a series of questions to stimulate discussion and guide participants to begin to question their personal experiences and common beliefs. As they question their assumptions and share new examples of ways of behaving, they begin to test general rules and principles that could be useful in their work. Such dialogues take time—from a few hours to several days—but they give valuable lessons and practice in formulating ethical positions and expressing them aloud in clear terms. This approach to critical reflection is incorporated into a curriculum called Youth Work Matters: Promoting Youth Development that we offer to youth-serving professionals through the Minnesota Youth Work Institute. The curriculum is taught in sessions totaling 24 hours by a team of skilled community youth workers and university-based faculty. It shares insights from the latest research by means of interactive, experiential activities, small-group work, accessible readings, stimulating debates, and mini-lectures.

Intentional ethical action

Intentional ethical action is the third step. This step involves developing skills to make decisions intentionally and solve problems in ethical ways in real life. An important piece about intentionality is that in order to do good youth work, we must always know why we do what we do. Ethically, nothing that we do with young people in our programs and in our practice should be happenstance or unintentional. We need to identify intended outcomes in our programs and our ways of working before we interact with youth, in order to meet youth needs accurately and effectively and be true to our ethos of positive youth development.

Let's go back to "The Pocket Knife Story." In terms of intentional action in youth work practice:

- What other basic need could the street worker focus on to diffuse the need for the knife?
- How does belief in the asset model help the street worker create positive options for the young man?
- How might the street worker and the youth work together to co-create a solution that makes the knife nonessential?

The "good kid–bad kid" scenario is an experiential activity that we use in our Youth Work Matters workshops to illustrate the implications and effects of unethical assumptions and biases of adults on young people. We create outlines of two youth—one labeled "good kid" and the other "bad kid." We ask participants to think of all the verbal, nonverbal, and visual cues that may be interpreted as making a young person good or bad and draw them on each outline. This activity visually guides practitioners to:

- Gain personal awareness of assumptions and biases we have about youth. For instance, why would horn-rimmed glasses indicate that the young person was probably a "good" kid? Why would sagging pants indicate that the young person was a "bad" kid?

- Critically reflect on our sometimes unethical assumptions and biases about youth and think about how these unexamined assumptions and stereotypes may dictate how we might unfairly treat and work with that young person.
- Be intentional about calling ourselves on these incongruent thoughts, words, and behaviors and create strategies to address them in our practice with youth.

Conclusion

Absent a formal code of ethical conduct for youth workers and community educators, we suggest using the stated ethos of positive youth development as a principle for practical ethical awareness, reflection, and intentional action. In creating professional development opportunities for adults working with youth, we encourage practitioners to reflect critically and be intentional about engaging youth and guiding them in developing and growing into healthy adulthood. Guiding youth in shaping their understanding of ethics is one component of this work.

Staff development opportunities can be designed to enable youth workers to explore their own ethos around youth development and learn ways of intentionally and authentically modeling and transmitting ethical values to youth in ways that meet basic youth needs. This idea of practice ethics can be incorporated in daily work with youth and in focused lessons to nurture ethical development in young people.

It really does matter that we practice what we preach with young people. The dilemmas of youth work practice vary from issues of pocket knives and speaking English to those of fair treatment and honorable behavior. As responsible adults, we are obligated not to sidestep these difficult and sometimes messy issues and are compelled ethically to take advantage of all our teaching moments.

Notes

1. Banks, S., & Nohr, K. (Eds.). (2003). *Teaching practical ethics for the social professions*. Odder, Denmark: Narayana Press. This was published by FESET (Formation d'Educateur Sociaux Europeens/European Social Educator Training). See http://www.feset.dk.

2. Kant, I. (1964). *Groundwork of the metaphysics of morals*. New York: Harper Collins.

3. Mill, J. S. (1972). *Utilitarianism, on liberty, and considerations on representative government*. London: Dent.

4. MacIntyre. A. (1985). *After virtue* (2nd ed.). London: Duckworth.

5. Gilligan, C. (1982). *In a different voice: Psychological theory and women's development*. Cambridge, MA: Harvard University Press.

6. Stone, B., Garza, P., & Borden, L. (2004). *Attracting, developing, and retaining youth workers for the next generation*. Report presented at the Wingspread Conference Proceedings, Nov. 16–18.

7. Walker, J., Marczak, M., Blyth, D., & Borden, L. (2005). Designing youth development programs: Towards a theory of developmental intentionality. In J. L. Mahoney, R. W. Larson, & J. S. Eccles (Eds.), *Organized activities as contexts of development: Extracurricular activities, after-school and community programs*. Mahwah, NJ: Erlbaum.

8. Konopka, G. (1973). Requirements for healthy development of adolescent youth. *Adolescence, 8*(31), 2–25.

9. Reimer, J., Paolitto, D. P., & Hersh, R. (1979). *Promoting moral growth: From Piaget to Kohlberg*. Prospect Heights, IL: Waveland Press.

10. Banks & Nohr. (2003).

11. Brookfield, S. (1989). Facilitating adult learning. In S. B. Merriam (Ed.), *Handwork of adult and continuing education* (pp. 201–210). San Francisco: Jossey-Bass.

12. Philippart, F. (2003). Using Socratic dialogue. In S. Banks & K. Nohr (Eds.), *Teaching practical ethics for the social professions*. Denmark: FESET, European Social Ethics Project.

13. Kohlberg, L. (1969). Stage and sequence: The cognitive-development approach to socialization. In D. A. Goslin (Ed.), *Handbook of socialization theory and research*. Skokie, IL: Rand McNally.

JOYCE A. WALKER *is a University of Minnesota professor and director of the Youth Development Leadership Masters of Education Program in the College of Education and Human Development.*

CECILIA F. GRAN *is the training coordinator for the Minnesota Youth Work Institute at the University of Minnesota.*

ARNOLDO CURIEL *is the diversity training coordinator for the Minnesota Youth Work Institute at the University of Minnesota.*

School-based character education tends toward a negative orientation (for example, preventing delinquency). Is there a better way to go—engaging the kinds of moral commitments exemplified by student activists?

2

Moral voices of politically engaged urban youth

Ben Kirshner

THE RELATIONSHIP BETWEEN reflection and action is an enduring question for those interested in promoting moral development among young people. Educators have struggled to find effective methods for educating youth to think carefully about moral problems and also show moral commitment in their everyday lives. Some have argued for cognitive approaches, which emphasize reasoning, judgment, and reflection, while others have argued for character-based approaches, which emphasize virtues such as honesty, loyalty, and integrity.[1]

Overlooked in these debates, however, are settings where young people engage in social justice action campaigns to improve their schools and communities. Such groups do not prioritize moral development as their goal. But by giving young people opportunities to combine moral judgment with action, they represent a promising approach to moral education, particularly for urban youth who are troubled by the inequities in their schools or lack of safe opportunities in their neighborhoods.

NEW DIRECTIONS FOR YOUTH DEVELOPMENT, NO. 108, WINTER 2005 © WILEY PERIODICALS, INC.

This chapter highlights the potential of youth activism to influence participants' moral and ethical development. What are the moral concerns that urban youth raise when given the opportunity? How do these concerns get translated into action? I summarize findings from moral development research and their relevance to youth engagement in social action and then draw on original and secondary sources to draw attention to the moral dimensions of social action campaigns organized by youth. This is not an empirical study, but instead an effort to bring attention to the moral perspectives raised by politically engaged youth.

Literature review: From moral reasoning to moral identity

Kohlberg's stages of moral development outlined transitions in children and adolescent's reasoning about moral dilemmas and inspired moral education programs focused on rational deliberation and discussion.[2] He found that young children make judgments primarily in self-interested terms—focusing on fear of punishment or desire for reward—but as they move into adolescence, they develop a greater appreciation for social conventions, such as the importance of maintaining order and respecting laws. Kohlberg also theorized a third level of reasoning, characterized by postconventional judgments based on principles of justice and human rights, but subsequent research found that few adults consistently reasoned this way.[3]

In recent years, approaches to moral education focused on Kohlberg's stages have been criticized on several levels. In addition to feminist and culturally based criticisms of Kohlberg's claim of universal stages, researchers have not been able to demonstrate a clear relationship between moral reasoning and behavior in real-life contexts.[4] Also, proponents of character education have argued that schools should return to an emphasis on a core set of moral virtues that focus on moral behavior and individual development but give less emphasis to discussions about social justice or broader social systems.[5]

Disenchantment with Kohlberg's theory, however, does not mean that educators should abandon the notion that reasoning is a critical feature of moral behavior. Sophisticated moral and political reflection is not limited to philosophers and educated elites; it is in fact central to informed participation in a democracy.[6] But how does reflection get united with action? How are we to think of moral behavior in a holistic way, taking into account a person's judgments, feelings, actions, and habits?

Efforts in this direction have led to the concept of moral identity, described by Hart, Atkins, and Ford as "a commitment consistent with one's sense of self to lines of action that promote or protect the welfare of others."[7] This notion is based on the premise that sustained moral action results only when people conceive of themselves and their goals in moral terms, in other words, when they identify with certain moral standards.[8] For the purposes of this chapter, I conceive of moral identity broadly, to include domains of political and civic participation as well, because they too are concerned with contributing to a broader social good.[9]

The concept of moral identity emphasizes adolescents as active interpreters of their world. Even young children interpret, evaluate, and reflect on messages communicated by parents and society and do not merely internalize external directives.[10] Also, moral identity takes into account the influence of social and cultural context.[11] Social context is especially salient when considering youth in low-income settings who must deal with inadequate resources, a lack of safety, and social prejudices. In their everyday lives, these youth encounter situations that touch on issues of justice, rights, and welfare.[12] It might prove to be productive for young people who are confronted with such problems to reflect on the fairness of such political and social arrangements and to consider strategies for improving the situation.

Research on moral identity formation suggests that adolescents' natural tendency to make meaning about their social surroundings should be the starting point for moral education. Yet many efforts at moral or character education in schools remain fragmented, cobbling together topics ranging from citizenship to teen sexuality, but with limited effort to draw connections among programs or relate them to students' lives. Furthermore, they often adopt a negative orientation, hoping to prevent delinquency, rather than appealing to students' strengths, hopes, and capacity for moral insight.[13]

Community-based social action projects, however, give youth the opportunity to confront social problems they observe in their everyday lives.[14] Unlike traditional models of community service, wryly dubbed "the lucky helping the needy" by Kahne and Westheimer, social action projects are oriented toward helping one's own community through influencing the deeper causes of problems.[15] Such projects give youth the opportunity to build leadership skills, develop their moral voices, and take action on issues they care about.

Moral voices

Here we look at four examples of moral voices about issues that concerned youth: reducing sexual harassment, creating enriching spaces, combating toxic pollution, and political organizing. The first case is based on my own research. The three others are drawn from analysis of published sources and brochures; I used these sources to examine how youth participants talked about and interpreted the issues that concerned them.

Reducing sexual harassment

The following two quotations reflect concerns raised by teenagers in SLASH (Student Leaders Against Sexual Harassment) about the prevalence of sexual harassment in their school:

Being a part of SLASH gives me an opportunity to help my community in an issue that I feel strongly about. Often times people see sexual harassment, but they don't do anything about it. . . . I know that SLASH will.

I joined SLASH because a lot of sexual harassment happens to everybody. It's not a good feeling and it's not a joke.

Although the statements reflect different levels of complexity, the two comments convey a moral standard that sexual harassment is wrong and reflect a sense of obligation to change the situation.

The teenagers in SLASH came together as part of an after-school program in Community Bridges Beacon (CBB), a youth organization in San Francisco's Mission District. Middle school and high school student participants were asked to determine a problem that they wanted to change in their community. After lengthy discussion and debate, the group chose sexual harassment among students as a prevalent problem in their schools. With the assistance of an adult facilitator, the students began a year-long project involving interviews with administrators, surveys of students, and research on district policy.

One CBB staff member described a powerful moment that took place when students talked with adults about the problem of sexual harassment. After hearing the opinion voiced that in essence, "there will always be youth who do such things," the students sought to find explanations of the problem that went beyond attributing blame solely to youth. SLASH eventually chose to investigate situations in which sexual harassment was tolerated in the school system. After examining survey data and school records, the students concluded that schools did not adequately educate youth and teachers about the issue and failed to ensure that existing rules were enforced. By the end of the year, SLASH had succeeded in persuading the San Francisco School Board to pass a resolution calling for a revision in its policies and procedures regarding sexual harassment. The group also sought to create greater awareness about the issue through multiple channels, including a youth conference at a local cultural center and a comic book/manual, *Sexual Harassment Hurts Everyone*, that was distributed to every student in the school district.

Creating enriching spaces

One of the young people growing up in Oakland, California, was quoted in this way in a report written by three teenagers chronicling the lack of opportunities for youth in Oakland:[16]

Here's a place where right is wrong and wrong is right. Every thing is backwards; then they wonder why there's a loss of respect because it was never given. You have to grow up fast just to keep up with our peers. Stepping out of your house is like stepping into another world. No love, not knowing who you can trust, and at any point in time anything can happen and will happen. . . . Elders look at me and think I'm a menace to society, but they do not know I'm doing the best I know how.

In the summer of 1996, a group of youth called Youth of Oakland United (YOU) surveyed two hundred youth about their general concerns. They used their findings to develop proposals for Oakland's City Council. Their report addressed the lack of safe, fun, and constructive places for youth to go after school and during the summer. According to the report, existing teen centers served fewer than two hundred teens each day, which was less than 1 percent of thirty-six thousand teens in Oakland.

The authors raised issues of justice and fairness in comparing the opportunities for youth in Oakland to those in the neighboring towns of Piedmont and Berkeley, saying, "recreation centers in Oakland look bad by comparison." Moreover, the youth centers that were in Oakland did not attract teenagers, for reasons ranging from their unsafe conditions to not engaging adolescent interests and opinions.

As a solution to this lack of opportunities, YOU proposed that Oakland provide funding for youth organizations that would meet the diverse interests and needs of young people. For example, some requested music instruction. Others requested workshops on how to interview for a job or get financial aid for college. Also, reflecting a concern similar to members of SLASH, the participants wanted these places to be safe: "The facilities should have peer conflict mediators to maintain a safe environment by resolving conflicts without violence."[17] Finally, youth felt that they should have a voice in the process of developing such opportunities. With the help of adult organizers and lawyers, the proposals articulated by YOU were drafted into a ballot initiative known as "Kids First" (Measure K), which called for 2.5 percent of the city budget to be directed toward after-school programs for Oakland youth. The ballot was approved in 1996 city elections.

Combating toxic pollution

A participant in a research project undertaken by thirteen year olds living in Richmond, California, asked, "How can they dump toxic chemicals into the bay? It gets into the fish and we get sick because we eat fish."[18] Richmond is an industrial city known for its disproportionate number of oil refineries, waste incinerators, and chemical manufacturers. The participants in this project, who came together under the auspices of the Asian Pacific Environmental Network (APEN), were Laotian girls whose families had immigrated to the United States. The goal of the project was for the participants to identify features of their local environments that promoted or inhibited their health. They found that several local waterways, including ones fished by Laotian residents for sustenance, were polluted by toxins from local industry.

As a result of their findings, the students made a number of public presentations. At the United Nations Environmental Youth Forum, the students articulated their findings about the lack of natural spaces and nontoxic gathering places in Richmond and made suggestions for what types of environments would be more positive for youth. On a local level, the participants held a community forum at which they explained to families and friends which waterways were polluted and the dangerous consequences of fishing there.

Mobilizing voters

In 2000 members of the Third Eye Movement, a group of politically active young people in California, fought the passage of Proposition 21, designed as a "get tough on crime" policy on juvenile crime. Proposition 21 increased the range of youth cases that could be tried in adult courts and the penalties for juvenile offenses. For example, it treated graffiti and other property damage costing more than four hundred dollars to repair as felonies, thus prosecutable under the "three strikes" mandate.[19]

The stated goal of the ballot initiative was to keep neighborhoods and schools safe. And as shown by members of SLASH, YOU, and APEN, safety was a critical issue for youth. But many young Californians interpreted Proposition 21 as detrimental to their safety and well-being rather than protective of it. For example, they wrote in a brochure, "Youth are not the enemy. But they treat us like we are. . . . The poverty, poor schools, racism and disrespect for young people in California is not our fault. . . . And now they're trying to pass an initiative to lock us all up and throw away the key, saying it'll make us safer. " Media reports documented the unexpected grassroots organizing among youth opposed to the initiative across the state.[20]

Youth activists offered several objections, including fears of being wrongfully targeted by police and criticism of the notion that a juvenile mistake should lead to an adult prison sentence. Also, some objected to what they perceived to be a hypocritical stance taken by policymakers, which blamed youth for society's problems but allocated few resources for improving their lives. They wondered why money was spent on a costly initiative when there did not seem to be enough money for public schools. As one youth opposed to the measure explained:

Walk into your school. . . .You'll see chipped paint. Wanna go to the bathroom? There's no toilet paper, no soap, no towels to wipe your hands on. Go up to your classroom. You have no books, or your books are limited to classroom use, or the books that are in the classroom are falling apart and the teacher says, "Here's a piece of tape so you can tape 'em up." Walk into another classroom and the teacher tells you to watch over your head because the ceiling is falling down and it won't be repaired for two weeks.[21]

By focusing on the failings of many inner-city public schools, the student activists framed the proposition as a social justice issue.

Opposition to Proposition 21 illustrates the finding from moral identity research that young people actively interpret policies and adult directives rather than just internalize them. Evidently young people had quite different conceptions of what it would take to ensure safety and well-being. Whereas policymakers sought to ensure safety through zero tolerance, youthful opponents argued that safety would be ensured through improved schools and community centers.

Who shapes the moral agenda for youth?

Writing in the 1960s, Erik Erikson suggested that criticism and renewal comprise a central task of adolescence: "In youth the tables of childhood dependence begin slowly to turn: no longer is it merely for the old to teach the young the meaning of life. It is the young who, by their responses and actions, tell the old whether life as represented to them has some vital promise, and it is the young who carry in them the power to confirm those who confirm them, to renew and regenerate, to disavow what is rotten, to reform and rebel."[22]

This chapter has highlighted four social action campaigns in which youth activists combine critical reasoning with moral action. Participants wrestled with essential moral notions of justice, rights, and welfare as they sought solutions to pressing problems. Student leaders in the Mission District of San Francisco found that large numbers of their peers felt vulnerable and unsafe in school; they asked school administrators to handle sexual harassment more forcefully and to promote education about the issue. Young women in Richmond appealed to notions of environmental justice; they asked why it was that they must live in a toxic area and sought healthy alternatives for their community. Youth in Oakland declared their rights to be safe, have fun, and develop career opportunities; they argued that it was unfair that youth in nearby towns had a greater number of such opportunities. Political activists across California questioned the moral integrity of a proposal to expand the reach of the criminal justice system into the lives of youth when large numbers of urban public schools were deteriorating.

Caveats

Although the youth quoted in this chapter reflect their concerns about social justice, this analysis is not meant to suggest that all young people share these views. Other research has shown that some youth blame themselves or their peers for problems they experience in their schools.[23] Also, this analysis did not attempt to identify the impact of participation on youth's moral development or evaluate different levels of reasoning. The understanding of some young people of these social issues may have been complex and nuanced, while that of others may have been more superficial.

Nevertheless, the examples underscore the potential of social action for the moral and civic development of youth and suggest directions for further research. For example, future studies might look into the conditions in which it is developmentally adaptive for youth living in distressed neighborhoods to reason critically about their social and political circumstances, especially when this reasoning is connected to action.

Implications for civic engagement

Some readers might interpret these four case studies as examples of a culture of oppositional youth who are angry at mainstream institutions and reject their norms and values. But this interpretation is not merited when one considers the desires and goals that motivated these projects. Certain themes were common: a desire for safe places, fun things to do, better educational opportunities, and clean neighborhoods. Far from radical or extreme, their demands reflect a basic wish to grow up in a healthy environment.

The examples also reflect youths' desire to participate in a larger world of civic institutions and democratic decision-making. In all four cases, youth brought their concerns to a wider, public platform. SLASH and YOU succeeded in persuading adults to pass resolutions that led to meaningful policy changes. Although Proposition 21 was eventually passed, opposition efforts mobilized a network of youth organizations for future civic engagement. Many of the youth talked about this being the first time they had a sense of their own power, especially in relation to political structures. For example, one of the youth fighting Proposition 21 said, "We're gonna get some new families into politics, instead of just the Kennedys, the Bushes, the Franklins, the Washingtons—the Manigos, the Ossorios!"[24]

The profiles discussed here underscore the value of community-based organizations. Such organizations are not always viewed as sites for moral education, perhaps because they rarely use the language of moral or character education to describe their goals. But they have great potential to support youth's burgeoning moral and political identities.[25] Flanagan and Faison write that such organizations offer "young people opportunities to explore what it means to be a member of 'the public', and to work out the reciprocity between rights and obligations in the meaning of citizenship."[26] Through engaged participation, urban youth take on responsible leadership roles and articulate their own questions and concerns about the larger democracy of which they are a part.

Conclusion

Youth activism represents a promising synthesis of two broad goals in moral education: the development of moral judgments about the social and political world and the ability to implement one's principles in action. Among working-class and poor youth, such commitments often take place in a context where inequities in resources, opportunities, and safety are salient, and thus discussions about justice, rights, and welfare are central features of moral and political identity development. Studying how youth assess and transform their local environments represents a promising direction for understanding moral development among adolescents in diverse social contexts. While some might regret that young people must fight for clean parks and safe schools, such struggles contribute to youth's moral development as well as the renewal of local communities and schools.

Notes

1. Bennett, W. J. (1991). Moral literacy and the formation of character. In J. S. Benninga (Ed.), *Moral, character, and civic education in the elementary school* (pp. 131–138). New York: Teachers College Press; Nucci, L. (2001). *Education in the moral domain.* Cambridge: Cambridge University Press; Tappan, M. B. (1998). Moral education in the zone of proximal development. *Journal of Moral Education, 27*(2), 141–161.

2. Kohlberg, L. (1976). Moral stages and moralization: The cognitive-developmental approach. In T. Lickona (Ed.), *Moral stages and moral behavior: Theory, research, and social issues* (pp. 31–53). New York: Holt.

3. Arnett, J. J. (2004). *Adolescence and emerging adulthood: A cultural approach.* Upper Saddle River, NJ: Prentice Hall.

4. Hart, D., & Fegley, S. (1995). Prosocial behavior and caring in adolescence: Relations to self-understanding and social judgment. *Child Development, 66,* 1346–1359; Gilligan, C. (1993). Adolescent development reconsidered. In A. Garrod (Ed.), *Approaches to moral development: New research and emerging themes.* New York: Teachers College Press; Shweder, R. (1995). Cultural psychology: What is it? In N. R. Goldberger & J. B. Veroff (Eds.), *The culture and psychology reader.* New York: New York University Press.

5. Bennett. (1991).

6. Turiel, E. (1989). Multifaceted social reasoning and educating for character, culture, and development. In L. Nucci (Ed.), *Moral development and character education: A dialogue* (pp. 161–182). Berkeley: McCutchan.

7. Hart, D., Atkins, R., & Ford, D. (1998). Urban America as a context for the development of moral identity in adolescence. *Journal of Social Issues, 54*(3), 515.

8. Damon, W., & Gregory, A. (1997). The Youth Charter: Towards the formation of adolescent moral identity. *Journal of Moral Education, 26*(2), 117–130.

9. Yates, M., & Youniss, J. (1996). A developmental perspective on community service in adolescence. *Social Development, 5*(1), 85–110.

10. Hart, D., & Killen, M. (1995). Introduction: Perspectives on morality in everyday life. In M. Killen & D. Hart (Ed.), *Morality in everyday life.* Cambridge: Cambridge University Press.

11. Haste, H. (1997). Lay social theory: The relation between political, social, and moral understanding. *New Directions in Child Development,* 27–38.

12. My definition of the moral domain is drawn from work by Turiel, Nucci, and colleagues, which shows that morality and social convention represent different developmental domains that are differentiated by individuals of all ages. Moral issues represent universally applicable truths, which are structured by underlying conceptions of justice, rights, and welfare. In contrast, social conventions are the arbitrary and agreed-on uniformities in social behavior determined by specific social systems. This discussion can be found in Nucci (2002).

13. Damon & Gregory. (1997).

14. Cervone, B. (2002). *Taking democracy in hand: Youth action for education change in the San Francisco Bay Area.* Providence, RI: What Kids Can Do & The Forum for Youth Investment.

15. Kahne, J., & Westheimer. J. (1996). In the service of what? The politics of service learning. *Phi Delta Kappan, 77*(9), 593–599; Sullivan, L. (1997). Hip-hop nation: The undeveloped social capital of black urban America. *National Civic Review, 86*(3), 235–243.

16. Ashley, J., Samaniego, D., and Cheun, L. (1997). How Oakland turns its back on teens: A youth perspective. *Social Justice, 24*(3), 170–177.

17. Ashley et al. (1997).

18. Schwab, M. (1997). Sharing power: Participatory public health research with California teens. *Social Justice, 24*(3), 11–32. See also Meucci, S., & Redmon, J. (1997). Safe spaces: California children enter a policy debate. *Social Justice, 24*(3), 139–152.

19. For nonpartisan information about the details of the law, see the Web site of the California state legislative analyst: http://www.lao.ca.gov/ballot/ 2000/21_03_2000.html.

20. Thompson, A. C. (2000, Feb. 9). Fighting the fearmongers. *San Francisco Bay Guardian*, 21–23. See also Kwon, S. A. (in press). Youth of color organizing for juvenile justice. In P. Noguera, S. Ginwright, & J. Cammarota (Eds.), *Youth, democracy and community change: New perspectives in practice and policy for America's youth*.

21. Thompson. (2000, Feb. 9).

22. Erikson, E. (1968). *Identity: Youth and crisis*. New York: Norton.

23. Kirshner, B. (2004). *Democracy now: Activism and learning in urban youth organizations*. Unpublished doctoral dissertation, Stanford University; Way, N. (1998). *Everyday courage: The lives and stories of urban teens*. New York: New York University Press.

24. Thompson. (2000, Feb. 9).

25. Ginwright, S., & James, T. (2002). From assets to agents of change: Social justice, organizing, and youth development. In B. Kirshner, J. L. O'Donoghue, & M. McLaughlin (Eds.), *Youth participation: Improving institutions and communities*. New Directions for Youth Development, no. 96, 27–46. San Francisco: Jossey-Bass.

26. Flanagan, C., & Faison, N. (2001). *Youth civic development: Implications of research for social policy and programs*. Ann Arbor, MI: Society for Research in Child Development. P. 7.

BEN KIRSHNER *is an assistant professor in education at the University of Colorado, Boulder.*

Unethical occurrences at major livestock shows have spurred the need to raise ethical awareness to youngsters involved in agriculture. The authors devised and evaluated an ethics curriculum for high school agriculture students.

3

Capitalizing on the human-animal bond to teach ethics to youth

Clinton P. Rusk, Keli M. Brubaker,
Mark A. Balschweid, Edmond A. Pajor

IN THE PAST DECADE, there have been several occurrences at major livestock shows where individuals have been caught breaking the rules. In 1994, eight exhibition animals were disqualified at the Ohio State Fair.[1] The 2003 Illinois State Fair disqualified the grand champion steer because of a drug violation.[2] There have also been instances of false ownership of animals, physical alteration of animals, and excessive involvement of professional livestock handlers.

These events prompt the question as to whether there is a need to raise ethical awareness along with other important aspects of raising livestock. *Ethics* refers to "the principles that define behavior as right, good and proper."[3] It also refers to what we believe is right and wrong, good and bad, or fair and unfair.[4]

Keith and Vaughn studied the value of competitive 4-H events as perceived by the parents of 4-H members.[5] The most common

NEW DIRECTIONS FOR YOUTH DEVELOPMENT, NO. 108, WINTER 2005 © WILEY PERIODICALS, INC.

problem identified by participants was excessive parental involvement. The second most common problem perceived by parents was unethical practices. Students involved in FFA were found to have similar perceptions of unethical practices in youth livestock programs.[6]

It is important that youth understand there is a much broader responsibility than individual honors, financial gain, or even individual misconduct. They must understand that the actions of a single competitor can affect the image of all youth involved in the livestock industry.

Theoretical framework

In order to eliminate unethical behavior, it is important to understand why people make the decisions they do. This study was based on Lawrence Kohlberg's theory of moral development, which is the increasing ability to differentiate and integrate the perspectives of self and others while making moral decisions.[7] Kohlberg's theory states that moral development is promoted by social experiences that produce cognitive conflict and provide a child with an opportunity to take the perspective of others. Kohlberg also contends that moral thinking can be advanced educationally using social interaction, cognitive conflict, a positive moral atmosphere, and democratic participation.

Purpose of the study

The purpose of this study was to evaluate the effectiveness of a livestock ethics curriculum developed for high school students in agricultural education classes. Mounce and Terry indicated a need for ethics education among agriculture students as a result of their study on the perceptions of unethical practices in FFA competitions.[8] Because of these unethical practices, livestock show officials have become more aware of the practices that exhibitors or their parents, or both, will engage in to win. In order to stop the unethical practices from occurring in any organization, education is needed.

The ethics curriculum for this research was developed, implemented, and evaluated to determine the effect of teaching ethics to high school youth in agricultural education programs. The following research questions were tested:

1. Are participants aware of the principles involved in making ethical choices in youth livestock programs?
2. Are participants able to determine whether certain practices at a youth livestock show are ethical or unethical?
3. Will participants make ethical choices in youth livestock programs as demonstrated by real-life case study analysis?
4. Will current grade in school; gender; years enrolled in 4-H; years enrolled in FFA; years enrolled in beef, swine, sheep, horse, dairy, and other livestock projects; or previous participation in a livestock ethics curriculum help explain the difference in pre- and posttest scores among participants?

Methodology

The study focused on advancing ethics education by developing a curriculum that involved student interaction, conflict, and a positive moral atmosphere. Tools used in the curriculum included a videotape, classroom discussion, and case scenarios.[9] Previous research has shown that an increase in ethical knowledge can result from a livestock ethics video program.[10] A pretest-posttest was used to measure knowledge gain. The second author administered the tests before and after teaching the curriculum, thus allowing students to receive detailed and consistent instructions on how to fill out the questionnaire.

Curriculum design

The curriculum began with a general overview of ethics. Students participated by answering questions and generating ideas on how to demonstrate ethical behavior in livestock programs and other areas of life. The Goodwin ethics video provided participants with decision-making tools to use when involved in livestock programs.[11]

Finally, students participated in case scenario evaluation. The cases were based on actual occurrences and described situations youth might face in the youth livestock program. Tomlinson suggested that dividing the scenario into the following steps—the situation, what happened next, and then what happened—is an effective way to help students learn.[12] Each part of the scenario featured discussion questions students could use while evaluating the situations.

Development of the instrument

The questionnaire was developed to measure knowledge gained from the ethics curriculum and identify whether students were able to evaluate a case scenario and make ethical choices. Participants were asked if they had ever participated in a livestock ethics curriculum. They were also asked to identify an example of an unethical situation involving livestock in order to determine their awareness of unethical practices occurring in the youth livestock program.

Twelve multiple-choice questions related to material covered during the instruction on ethics. Eight questions asked students to determine if a given response to a particular livestock situation was ethical or unethical. Students were also asked to list three of the four standard questions, developed by Goodwin, which can be used to determine whether a decision regarding livestock projects is ethical or unethical.[13] The final section of the pretest-posttest was a case scenario evaluation that allowed students to use the tools they learned to make ethical choices.

Pilot testing was conducted using an animal sciences class at a local high school. The second author taught the ethics curriculum to the agricultural science students and administered the same pretest and posttest that was to be administered during data collection. The purposes of the pilot testing were to validate the evaluation tools and identify any design flaws in the curriculum instruction. As a result of pilot testing, an additional case scenario was added to the curriculum.

Reliability for the instrument was tested using the Kuder-Richardson Formula 20 (KR20). The KR20 is a special case of Cronbach's alpha, for ordinal dichotomies. An alpha of .72 was obtained for the instrument used in this study.

Identification of participants

The participants were 305 agricultural education students from eight Midwest high schools participating in the study. The students were enrolled in either an Animal Science or Fundamentals of Agricultural Science and Business course at the time of the study. The schools in the study were selected because of their strong agriculture and livestock programs.

Data collection and analysis

Data comparing overall pretest-posttest scores were evaluated using a paired sample t-test. Data comparing individual questions on the pretest-posttest were evaluated using the McNemar test, which is a 2×2 classification table used to evaluate the difference between paired samples.[14]

Data were also compared between groups determined by the demographic data. Overall scores were compared using a repeated-measures analysis between subject groups over time. The change in time and any differences among groups were evaluated.

Results

Of the 305 students who participated in the instruction, only 268 subjects were included in the study, because 37 students were missing a pretest or a posttest due to absenteeism. There were 146 freshmen (54.5 percent), 53 sophomores (19.8 percent), 37 juniors (13.8 percent), and 32 seniors (11.9 percent) who participated in this study. Results from a repeated-measures analysis over time showed that all grade levels improved their test scores from the pretest to the posttest, but there was no significant difference between the grade levels.

There were 150 (56.0 percent) male participants and 118 (44.0 percent) female participants. Results showed that both males and females improved their test scores from the pretest to the posttest, but there was no significant difference between the two groups.

The mean number of years enrolled in 4-H for participants who had at least one year of 4-H enrollment (n = 115) was 5.03 years. The mean number of years of FFA membership for those students who had at least one year of FFA enrollment (n = 135) was 1.79 years. Participants who had previously been enrolled in 4-H or FFA had higher scores, F (1, 266) = 62.4, p < .001, than those who had not been previously enrolled in 4-H or FFA. Although there was a difference in scores between groups, the amount of change over time was similar for the two groups.

Individuals who had previously been enrolled in an animal project had higher scores, F (1, 266) = 44.7, p < .001, than those who had not been previously enrolled in an animal project. Although there was a difference in scores between groups, the amount of change over time was similar for the two groups.

The mean pretest score for was 17.82 correct answers out a possible 29 questions (61.45 percent) with a standard deviation of 3.5. Scores ranged from 6 to 25 correct answers. The posttest mean score was 21.07 correct answers (72.66 percent), with a standard deviation of 3.6. Scores ranged from 8 to 27 correct answers. Figure 3.1 shows the distribution of pretest and posttest scores of all participants. The results indicate an 18 percent gain (t = −18.583, p < 0.05) in student knowledge of livestock ethics as a result of the curriculum, which is 3.26 correct responses. Eighty-six percent of participants improved their score from the pretest to the posttest.

Prior to instruction, 41.6 percent of the participants were able to identify at least one example of an unethical practice related to the youth livestock program. Following instruction, 93.6 percent were able to list an unethical practice involving the youth livestock program.

As noted in Table 3.1, there was an improvement in the number of correct answers from the pretest to the posttest on all but one of

Figure 3.1. Distribution of the number of correct answers on the pretest and posttest

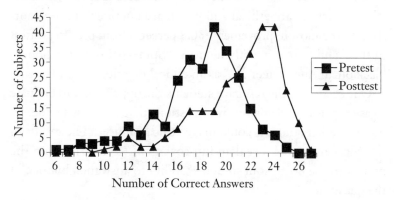

Table 3.1. Percentage of correct answers by participants on statements used to identify ethical or unethical practices

Statement	Pretest	Posttest	P-value
1. Hiring a professional groomer to prepare your animal the day of the show while you stand back and watch. . .	80.9	68.9	<.001
2. Walking your calves thirty minutes each day to prepare them for show day. . .	92.2	97.0	<.05
3. Spray-painting the hooves black on an Angus steer. . .	22.6	53.4	<.001
4. Using a water hose to fill up your barrow in order to make the minimum weight requirement. . .	86.2	93.3	<.001
5. Withholding feed and water from your pig two days before the show in order to meet the maximum weight requirement. . .	89.6	93.3	<.05
6. Teaching your lamb to stand firmly at a young age in order for it to perform better during showmanship. . .	91.8	97.4	<.001
7. Rubbing mud on ringworm spots on a lamb before it goes through the health inspection at the fair. . .	94.4	96.6	>.05
8. Washing a cow to give her a shiny appearance on show day. . .	96.3	99.6	<.01

Note: Questions 1, 4, 5, and 7 are unethical practices.
Questions 2, 3, 6, and 8 are ethical practices.

the eight livestock-related practices that participants were asked to identify as either ethical or unethical. The table footnote identifies which practices are ethical and which are unethical. Participants showed the most improvement (30.8 percent) from pre- to posttest in their ability to correctly identify, "Spray-painting the hooves black on an Angus steer . . ." as an ethical practice.

One section of the test gave students the opportunity to evaluate a case scenario and answer five questions that were used to determine whether students could make ethical choices. The results of the McNemar test reveal an improvement ($p < .001$), from the pretest to the posttest in students' ability to answer all but one of the questions.

Interpreting the knowledge gains

The first objective of this study was to increase participants' awareness of the principles involved in making ethical choices in youth livestock programs. Participants increased their awareness and knowledge of the principles involved in making ethical choices by 18 percent. A majority (86 percent) of participants improved their score from the pretest to the posttest. These results show that most high school–aged students are capable of learning how to make ethical choices. With the reported rise in cheating, stealing, and lying over the past ten years among high school students, there is obviously a need for ethics education at the high school level, and maybe even earlier.[15]

The second objective was to assess whether a livestock ethics curriculum helped students determine whether certain practices at a youth livestock show are ethical or unethical. After receiving the ethics curriculum, 52 percent more participants were able to list an unethical practice associated with the youth livestock program. By applying Goodwin's four "ethical compass" questions—Does the practice violate Food and Drug Administration law? Does the practice harm the animal? Does the practice fraudulently misrepresent the animal? Does the practice have anything to do with real-world agriculture?—participants were better able to determine whether seven of the eight situations were ethical or unethical.[16]

The third objective of the study was to identify whether participants would make ethical choices in youth livestock programs as demonstrated by real-life case study analysis. After analyzing several case scenarios, students were better able to identify the decisions being made, determine which aspects of the scenario were ethical, and make an ethical choice when asked to decide what the character in the scenario should do.

The final objective of the study was to determine if grade in school; gender; years enrolled in 4-H, FFA, beef, swine, sheep, horse, dairy, and other livestock projects; or previous participation in a livestock ethics curriculum help explain the difference in pre- and posttest scores among participants. The data showed that past enrollment in 4-H, FFA, or an animal project and the ability to list an unethical practice resulted in higher pre- and posttest scores than those who had no previous enrollment. The remainder of the demographic characteristics had no effect on the results.

Limitations

There was a significant decrease from the pretest to the posttest scores in students' ability to determine if the following situation was ethical or unethical: "Hiring a professional groomer to prepare your animal the day of the show while you stand back and watch." This result points out the limitation of using "correct answers" on a test to measure ethics. The decrease in correct answers on this situation may be due to insufficient detail being presented during instruction of the curriculum or simply a misunderstanding of the material presented. In either case, measuring ethics based on correct answers on a test has its limitations. There is no guarantee that participants will make ethical choices in actual situations. Further research needs to be done to determine whether the participants from this study do make ethical choices when given an opportunity to apply the skills they learned from the ethics curriculum.

Even after completing the ethics curriculum, 46.6 percent of participants thought the practice of spray-painting the hooves black on an Angus steer was unethical. This result was in spite of the videotape (used in the curriculum) presenting a visual comparison of spray-painting hooves to washing and waxing the tires on an automobile before it is sold. Spray-painting an animal's hooves makes it look prettier but does not change the animal's conformation. Thus, painting hooves is an ethical practice, yet nearly half of the participants failed to learn this during this ethics training.

Twenty-one of the 268 students indicated they had been through a previous ethics training program. We expected these individuals to score higher on the pre- and posttest than those with no previous ethics training. However, there was no difference in the pre- and posttest scores of these students. These results could be due to the low number of participants who had been through previous ethics training, or possibly due to participants' not having an opportunity to apply the knowledge they learned from previous ethics training. If the knowledge was not applied, students may have forgotten the principles involved in making ethical choices. If the participants in this study do not have an opportunity to make ethical choices in real-life situations, they may lose the knowledge they gained from this curriculum.

Further research is warranted to determine if an ethics curriculum can be developed and implemented in school classrooms or in after-school programs. Longitudinal studies are also needed to determine whether teaching an ethics curriculum can make a long-term change in student behaviors and improve their ability to make ethical choices.

Implications

The students who were taught the livestock ethics curriculum had a better understanding of the ethics associated with the youth livestock program, were more aware of the principles involved in making ethical choices when faced with decisions, and had a better understanding of the consequences of an unethical choice. Participants in this study are more likely to make an ethical choice when faced with a decision in the youth livestock program than they were prior to receiving the ethics curriculum.

The results of this study should be encouraging to those who work with youth, regardless of whether they work in a school or after-school setting. The fact that high school–aged students can learn how to make ethical choices is a positive sign. According to Kohlberg, people have a harder time learning ethics as they get older.[17] The assumption can be made that elementary and junior high students can also learn how to make ethical decisions, but further research needs to be conducted to verify this assumption.

The other interesting fact from this study is that even students who did not have an animal background improved their scores by an average of 12.8 percent on the posttest after being taught the livestock ethics curriculum. These students did not score as well as those who had previous animal experience, but their level of improvement from the pretest to the posttest was similar. Once again, the message is that students can learn how to make ethical choices if they are properly taught an ethics curriculum. The fact that the average score on the pretest was below 70 percent demonstrates the need for ethics training and the development of additional ethics curricula.

Students in mainstream America might benefit from an ethical compass similar to the one Goodwin developed for livestock practices.[18] A statement or set of questions that students could use to determine whether a decision they are about to make is ethical or unethical could be helpful.

Notes

1. Moser, L. (2003). Ohio livestock tampering law may set the framework for other states. *Hoard's Dairyman, 148*, 721–722.

2. Wills, C. (2003, Aug. 13). Illinois State Fair disqualifies teenager, champion steer for using banned drug. Retrieved August 21, 2003, from http://edition.cnn.com/2003/US/Midwest/08/13/offbeat.steer.scandal.ap/.

3. Josephson, M. (2002). *Making ethical decisions.* Marina del Ray, CA: Josephson Institute of Ethics.

4. Rollin, B. E. (1995, Dec.). *The ethics of livestock showing.* Paper presented at the LCI National Youth Livestock Program Ethics Symposium, Las Vegas, NV.

5. Keith, L., & Vaughn, P. (1998). The value of 4-H competitive activities as perceived by the parents of 4-H members. *Journal of Agricultural Education, 39*(3), 41–50.

6. Mounce, A. R., & Terry, R., Jr. (2001, Jan.). *Students' perceptions of unethical practices in FFA competitions.* Paper presented at the Southern Agriculture Education Conference, Fort Worth, TX. Retrieved January 22, 2003, from http://aaaeonline.ifas.ufl.edu/Research percent20Conferences/Saerc/2001/pdf/a3.pdf.

7. Kohlberg, L. (1969). Stage and sequence: The cognitive-developmental approach to socialization. In D. A. Golsin (Ed.), *Handbook of socialization theory and research* (pp. 347–480). Skokie, IL: Rand McNally.

8. Mounce & Terry. (2001, Jan.).

9. Goodwin, J. (Producer). (1996). *The line in the sand* [Motion picture]. (Available from Texas A&M University, Mail Stop 2588, College Station, TX 77843–2588.)

10. Goodwin, J. L., Briers, G., & Murphy, T. H. (2002). Measuring the ethical cognition effects of a videotape livestock show ethics education program. *Journal of Extension, 40*(6). Retrieved from http://www.joe.org/joe/2002 december/rb2.shtml. Rus, D. G. (1997). *Evaluation of ethics perceptions in FFA members.* Unpublished master's thesis, Colorado State University, Fort Collins.

11. Goodwin. (1996).

12. Tomlinson, T. (1996). Constructing case studies for ethics teaching. *Ag Bioethics Forum, 8*(2), 7.

13. Goodwin et al. (2002).

14. *SPSS Version 11.5 for Windows* [Computer software]. (2000). Chicago: SPSS.

15. Josephson Institute of Ethics. (2002). *Report card 2002: The ethics of American youth.* Los Angeles: Author.

16. Goodwin. (1996).

17. Kohlberg. (1969).

18. Goodwin et al. (2002).

CLINTON P. RUSK *is an associate professor of youth development at Purdue University.*

KELI M. BRUBAKER *is a 4-H youth development educator in White County, Indiana.*

MARK A. BALSCHWEID *is an associate professor of agricultural education at Purdue University.*

EDMOND A. PAJOR *is an associate professor of animal sciences at Purdue University.*

The author examines the thinking and behavior of adolescents within the digital world—an environment that is largely not mediated by adults—and considers the applicability of the literature on youth ethics that is based on more traditional contexts.

4

Internet lives: Social context and moral domain in adolescent development

Karen Bradley

CLAIRE IS A JUNIOR in high school.[1] She has a virtual life, an existence online that forms a crucial part of her day and, perhaps, her identity. Claire spends hours every day instant messaging (IM) her friends and reading and writing blogs in what have come to be called "social networks" on the Internet. "I have a schedule," Claire says. "When I get up in the morning I check [my IM and selected blogs]; when I come home from school I check and before I go to sleep I check; but there are times in between I can check it too." Diana, a classmate of Claire, adds, "I have four e-mail addresses but I don't use them much. I use them for different things, but if I want to say something, I IM or blog." These adolescents leave their computers turned on and logged in to their instant messaging programs and blogging Web sites for days at a time. They socialize, network, and sort out their friendships and relationships online. They help each other with their homework online.

NEW DIRECTIONS FOR YOUTH DEVELOPMENT, NO. 108, WINTER 2005 © WILEY PERIODICALS, INC.

What does all this instant messaging and blogging after school hours mean? Why do adolescents do it? How much time do they spend doing it? How does it shape their social, emotional, and moral development? This chapter describes the phenomenon and explores some moral development ramifications of a new context of social experience for adolescents. It proposes that the digital world creates its own social context, with a different set of social conventions from the adult-mediated "real" world that adolescents also inhabit. It is a social context that most adults are aware of but do not understand. Adolescents' experiences in the online world influence their experiences in the face-to-face world and play an important role in their development of social and moral knowledge.

Theoretical context

In order to understand what is meant by the term *online social context*, it is helpful to situate it within moral development theory. Domain theory, a refinement of the child moral development theories pioneered by Jean Piaget and Lawrence Kohlberg, was developed in the 1980s by the American social psychologist Elliot Turiel and has since become widely, although not by any means universally, accepted among developmental psychologists, philosophers, and educators.

Piaget and Kohlberg pioneered the notion that morality "can be considered a developmental process" that emerges from a child's experiences of rules and punishments imposed on them by adults and from different forms of social experience and interaction. Piaget focused on moral development in young children, arguing that children move from a heteronomous moral thinking, in which rules are given to them and reinforced by punishment from adults, to an autonomous moral stage, in which they internalize many of the adult-given rules but also make independent moral judgments based on their social experiences.[2]

Kohlberg refined Piaget's work, studying moral development more longitudinally. Like Piaget, he concluded that moral knowledge is constructivist, emerging from a child's interactions in the social world and from accommodation and internalization of instructions transmitted by adults. Like Piaget, Kohlberg found that young children are concrete moral thinkers and develop an understanding of why conventional morality is good for society as they mature. Unlike Piaget, Kohlberg thought this process was gradual and lasted a lifetime. He posited three moral levels—pre-conventional, conventional, and postconventional—and six moral stages that fit within those levels.

In the 1980s, Elliot Turiel and his colleagues observed that the stage theory did not work as neatly in real life as it did in theory, because children appeared to be inconsistent in their moral decisions. Out of these observations came domain theory. Domain theory posits that the moral domain is one of several domains of thought and that moral decisions usually involve assessing and negotiating more than one domain. He suggested that there are actually three domains of thought: moral, social, and personal. These domains develop from the fact that children are challenged by different forms of social experience and quickly learn to categorize them differently. Over time, through interaction with others, they develop knowledge about themselves, society, and morality.

Children's social knowledge, for example, is obtained "through their participation in social groups, such as the family, school, or with their peers," Turiel explained. "Children form conceptions about social systems and the conventions, the shared expectations, that coordinate interaction."[3] So a preschooler quickly understands that in one class, the convention is to sit in a circle and sing a song in Japanese, "*Ité daki mas*" (Japanese for "now we can have our tea"), before snack time, whereas in another class at the same school, a snack is always available and she can get a piece of orange or pretzel whenever she feels like it. Different rules govern different social contexts and form social convention. As children get older, their moral thinking in action, their judgments about what is the "right" or "wrong" action in a given situation, develop in part from an understanding that social conventions are important to the smooth functioning of society but they are not intrinsically moral.[4] Realizing this might help parents to understand why so many teenagers ignore speed limit and drinking age laws: teenagers know speeding and drinking are wrong, but many of them can see no intrinsic harm in disobeying what they see as social convention.

The moral domain is different. Because, for example, the pre-schooler can observe the harm of pushing someone down (the person cries), he also understands that it is morally wrong to push, no matter what the context. Turiel's further explanation is helpful. "Moral prescriptions are not relative to the social context, nor are they defined by it," he writes. . . . "Children's moral judgments are . . . derived . . . from features inherent to social relationships—including experiences involving harm to persons, violations of rights, and conflicts of competing claims. . . . Moral prescriptions are *obligatory*. They are *universally applicable* in that they apply to everyone in similar circumstances. They are *impersonal* in that they are not based on individual preferences of personal inclinations."[5]

Turiel defines as fundamental moral thinking that which Kohlberg might have called postconventional thinking. Moral thinking is based on judgments of fairness, harm, or welfare that are a priori judgments. In other words, they do not depend on their social contexts.

Thus, according to domain theory, moral and social thought are distinct and parallel developmental frameworks that must be coordinated in real-world situations. As Turiel explained, "many situations calling for a behavioral decision of a moral nature also include non-moral social components that impinge on the decision-making process. . . . Behavior in such situations is not based solely on an application (or lack of application) of moral considerations, but would be related to the coordination of different domains of judgments."[6]

Depending on his or her accumulated interpretation of interactions in social contexts, together with the body of rules and instructions received from adults, a young person will weigh the social and moral implications presented by a given situation and use information from both the social and the moral domains to guide his decision-making process. Because individuals' accumulations of social interactions are so varied, different individuals will make different moral judgments in response to the same situation. Turiel showed, in short, that young people's ethical understandings involve ongoing attempts to "coordinate their social and normative understandings from several domains [of thought] simultaneously."[7]

The paradigm shift we have seen in the past twenty-five years has created an entirely new social context. It is located on the Internet. It is a social context involving instant messaging, social networking Web sites like MySpace.com and Xanga.com, blogging sites like Live-Journal and Fandom.net, and other virtual communities that appeal to the interests of adolescents. There is a thriving world of online fan clubs, dozens devoted to Harry Potter alone, for example: a perusal of the Web site "Leaky Cauldron," an adolescent favorite, provides a glimpse of what is available. Thousands of pages of fan fiction are self-published daily, as a glance at FanFiction.net will attest, and thousands of pages more of commentary on the fiction are generated as well. Many teenage boys gravitate to techie Web sites like Appe-x.net and Slashdot, online video gaming and poker, and sites that gather fan communities of those activities. Adolescents of both sexes love music sites, both legal and illegal, and share information, downloads, and technical tips. Some people claim that over 50 percent of the articles in the open online encyclopedia *Wikipedia* are written by high school students. It is enormous. It is buzzing, it is a world unto itself, and it qualifies as a separate social context because it has rules and etiquette, is enormously important to adolescents, and, unlike almost every other aspect of adolescent life, is not mediated by adults.

Characteristics of the digital social context

Autonomy, playfulness, seriousness, and intense learning characterize this new digital territory, which is used by more than 75 percent of people ages twelve to seventeen.[8] It is not bounded by traditional physical boundaries. Inside, online adolescent relationships are qualitatively different from face-to-face ones. The online world has its own etiquette, its own system of rules, and its own morality. Some exploration of these characteristics helps us to understand why it is a separate social context and how it plays a role in shaping the social and moral knowledge of young people.

Adolescence is marked by the desire for autonomy and independence. The Internet generally, and online social networking opportunities in particular, help adolescents feel autonomous. The Internet offers adolescents social, moral, recreational, and intellectual experiences that are not mediated by adults. The beauty of the Internet, to some, lies in its low barriers to entry: all one needs is a computer to "serve" information to the world, an Internet service provider (ISP), and the know-how to create Web sites. Many sites, such as the Harry Potter fan site SugarQuill.net and the student study aids site http://www.invadersrealm.com/, exist on user donations, which pay for servers and connection time. Some of the social networking Web sites were originally created by college students for college-age and teenage users. LiveJournal, for example, one of the most popular adolescent blogging and social networking sites, was created by University of Washington computer science major Brad Fitzpatrick in 1999; the popular college social networking site Facebook.com was created by Harvard undergraduates Mark Zuckerberg, Dustin Moskovitz, Andrew McCollum, and Chris Hughes in 2004. Other sites, created by adults with profits in mind, collect information about users to sell to advertisers, but the adult presence is unobtrusive to young users, constantly cycling advertisements notwithstanding.[9] To most teenage denizens of these digital communities, there are no adults, no rules, and no restrictions.

A second unique and appealing characteristic of the online social context from the adolescent perspective is that it is not constrained by traditional physical boundaries. People can become friends even if they cannot see one another; they are not limited by physical characteristics such as good looks, race, or age; they do not have to be inhibited by the shyness or social awkwardness they feel in the face-to-face world. In fact, for teenagers who are shy or socially awkward, the control over communication offered to them by instant messaging or blogging can be enormously empowering. "It's a lot easier to [explain yourself] when you have time to compose your thoughts than to do it on IM or in person or on the phone," says one sixteen-year-old girl. According to a 2001 Pew Internet and American Life study, "many teens feel less inhibited when using IM to talk to others, and in fact, 48 percent of online teens say that using the Internet to communicate has improved their relationship with friends, 32 percent claim it has helped them to make new friends, and 37 percent admit to saying something over IM they would not have said in person."[10] As one teenager puts it, "I'll feel really close to this person [because of what we talk about online], and then see them the next day at school and they'll just be like completely as if I don't exist." Another said, "Sometimes when I have a particularly breakthrough conversation [online] with someone we'll never actually address what we discussed [face-to-face], we'll just give each other an understanding look, but that's as far as it will go." Young people feel empowered by the different boundaries offered by the communication that happens online, freedom from physical characteristics, and the fact that the communication happens in a peer community.

Adolescents enjoy thinking of the Internet as a separate world from what they call the "real" world, and they see themselves and their friendships as having unique online identities and codes of behavior. "The time I spend on the Internet doesn't affect my real life at all and when it does it's weird," explains Diana. "Maybe reading fan fiction affects how I think about writing. But the way I interact with people . . . it's really not similar to the way I interact with them in real life." Kristin, a thoughtful seventeen year old, adds, "It's like you have an online personality and like a real personality. . . . There's a code of trust and you have to keep the things in the Internet on the Internet." "Yeah," says Maya, an outgoing high school senior. "It's a code of silence."

Nonetheless, the boundaries between the online and "real" world are in fact porous and constantly shifting. "Do people actually meet face-to-face if they are MySpace friends?" I ask my teenage interviewees. The answers vary and point to some of these permeable and changing boundaries. Some adolescents say that they never give online acquaintances "friends" privileges—access to personal blogs and instant messaging connection—unless they know them in person. Others say that the whole fun of sites like MySpace and Facebook is to collect online friends, whether they know them personally or not. Some teenagers collect over a hundred "friends" on their site, openly acknowledging that the "real" identity of some of their Internet friends could well be fictional. That is part of the fun, they say. They almost never meet, or want to meet, their Internet-only friends in person. It would be weird to meet an online friend in the "real" world, they say. But a significant component of young people's social interactions online are actually taking place with people they *do* know in the real world, and the effects of those interactions inevitably bleed across to the "real" world, informing young people's thinking in the social and moral domains.

Navigating the shoals of friendships and romantic relationships can be easier online, many teens think, because the online approach allows them to take emotional risks that do not feel quite as perilous. These online "practice sessions" play a critical role in young people's moral and social development for the face-to-face world as well. For example, it has become more and more common for people to assess romantic interest through online communication and ask for first dates online. Being able to assess dating interest online makes things easier, they say. Harvard undergraduate Olivia Ma confirms that instant messaging gives young people confidence: "Toby Poston, a sixteen-year-old high school junior from Savannah, GA., logs onto the Internet regularly to chat with friends and family," Ma writes. "He agrees that the less intimidating form of conversation definitely has advantages when it comes to doing things like asking for a girl's number. 'It's an easier let down,' [Poston] explained."[11] Alex, a college senior, confirms that instant messaging via Facebook has become standard operating procedure for establishing relationships at her university. "It's easier to ask somebody their e-mail than their phone number," echoes Maya, who is a full four years younger than Alex, "and it's easier to e-mail somebody than phone because if you call somebody and they're not interested in you it's going to be really awkward, but if you e-mail them and they never write back it's just kind of disappointing." To be left hanging by an unanswered e-mail feels much less hurtful than receiving a voice-to-voice or face-to-face rejection. "You're not putting yourself out there as much," says Diana. "It doesn't feel the same way to be open online as in person" she says:

These same people [with whom I am emotionally open with online] I would feel terrified to come up to them in person and start this kind of conversation. I want to and I think it would be more meaningful but it's just really scary, whereas on the Internet it's, like, they can just go away. If you write out your question and you press the "send" button and they just don't say anything if they don't want to talk to you they can just go away and your relationship is still intact. But if you come up to them in person and they feel like it was out of place and if they're a volatile person then they might storm off and never speak to you again.

And breakups? Those happen online too, but they are frowned on. They go against the rules of digital social etiquette.

There are not many rules in the online world, but there is an important moral dimension to how adolescents think about online activities: the "rules" of online conduct are defined by the interactions young people personally experience or hear about from their peers. It is an approach that makes light of adult-defined social conventions and tradition but preserves a basic sense of morality. In other words, the online social context allows young people to explore social knowledge relatively free of social convention but informed by moral thinking. They are able to do this because, as Turiel explained, "Moral prescriptions are . . . universally applicable." They do not depend on their social contexts.[12] Young people delight in the universe of information available to them online— the good, the bad, and the ugly, as some of them describe it—but see themselves as thoughtful, moral consumers able to make good decisions about what they read and do online.

Adult fears of rampant bullying and sexual harassment online, while not baseless, are overblown. Adolescents actively protect their privacy and identity, consider the implications of online "flaming," and feel protected by the code of silence that binds them to one another in the online world. For example, a recent study conducted by the Children's Digital Media Center at Georgetown University found that only one in five teenage bloggers offered his or her full name.[13] Most of the teenagers I interviewed confessed to having lied about their age when they registered for instant messaging or social networking sites. Discerning a person's real identity from a user name and biographical information that is at least in part fabricated is a challenge. Journalist Bob Sullivan acknowledged that in spite of his best efforts to find otherwise, "experts interviewed for [his] article could not cite a single case of a child predator hunting for and finding a child through a blog."[14]

Contrary to popular perception, adolescents generally do not engage in behavior online that flies in the face of most sexual and behavioral conventions.[15] We can see this in how gender relationships and conflicts are played out online. Adolescents relish the visual possibilities of blogs and use them to express creative interests, explore sexuality, and initiate romantic and sexual relationships. But most adolescents are careful about what they post. Girls, in particular, take pleasure in posting pictures of themselves in digital disguise. Boys are more likely to post undisguised pictures of themselves on social networking sites than girls are, although younger girls more than older girls send pictures of themselves to e-mail addresses of social network members they think are good looking (or whose digital identity is attractive).[16]

Since adolescent perceptions of social conventions about sexuality and violence, which they derive as much from popular culture as from role modeling in families and schools, are not all positive, however, the lack of adult mediation of the online world may allow cruel and exploitative behavior to take place unchallenged. Some teenagers I interviewed suggested that one downside to online social networking is that it allows sexual activity to begin earlier, in middle school for an increasing number of adolescents. They explained the phenomenon by saying that some boys are more daring in sexually propositioning girls online and that girls agree because they want to be "cool." In interviews where adolescents unanimously acclaimed the online social world, this was the one aspect of it that made most of them uneasy. But in an era in which young people are exposed to explicit sexuality through television and film at such early ages in ways that are also disturbing to adults, it is hardly surprising that their sexual exploration filters into the digital social context in ways that are ultimately disturbing, to both teens and their parents, as Benoit Denizet-Lewis so vividly illustrated in his 2004 article "Friends, Friends with Benefits and the Benefits of the Local Mall."[17]

As a medium for expressing anger and resolving conflict, the online world reflects moral and social thought of other social contexts, although the immediacy and accessibility of instant messaging sometimes allow anger to become groupthink explosions that can wreak long-term damage on a school community or social network. Interestingly, social knowledge in this area is changing rapidly. Most young people now know the perils of "flaming" online where many of them saw instant messaging as a free-for-all for rude behavior as few as three years ago. This social knowledge has developed quickly because of firsthand experience or stories of others' experiences of intense social cruelty or outright antisocial behavior playing out online. It also has developed because teenagers have experienced some of their online interactions reaching into and having a powerful impact on face-to-face ones in ways they did not intend and could not control.

Digital etiquette now suggests that while blogs and instant messaging conversations are great places to vent frustration and anger, anger against a particular person should be cryptically rendered. As one girl put it, "There have been times on my blog when I've said things about people who read my blog but I've just tried to make them so cryptic that they wouldn't understand." "Why do it in a blog instead of on paper?" I ask. Adolescents say it feels good just to have an audience, to let your readers know you are "pissed about *something*." And "in some ways it's kind of nice to know that other people will see it because you know that the person [to whom the explanation is directed] can't do something really unjustified because you know that other people are watching. So it's actually safe." And, another adds, if you need to, "you can actually print out the conversation and post it." Sometimes young people even print out a particularly disturbing instant message conversation or blog entry and show it to an adult. Adolescents now also understand that there is always a risk that an instant message conversation or a posting to a blog could be misinterpreted by a peer or read by an adult. The etiquette of adolescent blogging and instant messaging, in short, has rules about what is right and wrong, and while these conform in certain ways to social convention in the face-to-face world, they also create their own, more flexible conventions. It is a social context where the sense of right and wrong is in constant negotiation.

Experimentation and playfulness, hallmarks of the online world, go hand in hand with a techno-savvy amorality that flies in the face of real-world values and laws. Some say that because the Internet is freedom of speech incarnate, anything goes for anyone. As Mark, a seventeen-year-old boy, put it, "It's a haven of filth, but I love it . . . it . . . can't and should not be changed." The fact that exploitative people and those who sell guns and information about how to make bombs also use the Internet is "not the way it should be," he says. But freedom of information means that good and bad people get to use the Internet. Teenagers feel that, in general, they are "good" users of the Internet. Interestingly, however, they frequently break intellectual property laws without giving their actions much thought: the very anonymity of the Internet fosters the belief among them that actions that do not result in observable harm are de facto okay. Widespread "borrowing" results: of images, text, software, and, more than anything else, music.

While the online social context is playful and experimental, allowing adolescents to explore a variety of personas, it is also very serious. Teens work out conflicts, confess sexual identity online, and explore issues like depression and eating disorders when it is not safe to do so in the real world. Teenagers who feel alienated by their real-world communities often find communities online. As one seventeen-year-old girl explained,

The Internet does provide you with a community that is larger than what you see. When I was . . . experimenting with my sexuality I was like I don't know anyone at school who I [could] talk to about this. But like you go online and you see like "how to talk to your friends if you think you might be bisexual." You realize that there's a larger world out there that you don't have to feel like oh no I'm a freak and so it provides you with a larger sense of perspective and that's really helpful.

An enormous amount of learning takes place online. Adolescents can develop interests that their parents' generation simply could not. Adolescents can also learn a lot more about what their parents' generation might consider "illicit" or "age inappropriate" than the parents ever could have, in spite of the existence of filters and blockers on family computers. This includes information about sex and sexuality, alternative cultures, and drugs and is a source of enormous concern for some parents. Some parents try to deal with their adolescent children's budding interests by helping them become critical and careful users of the Internet; others try to control the information to which their teenage children gain access.

In the most prosaic and powerful way, the online social context is important because nearly every adolescent inhabits it. Virtually all teens have access to the Internet, whether at home, school, libraries, cafés, or friends' houses. The results of "Teenage Life Online: The Rise of the Instant Message Generation," a 2001 study by the Pew Internet and American Life Project, reveal that some 74 percent of the 17 million teens online in 2001 were into instant messaging.[18] Today, about one-third to one-half of teens also actively blog.[19] It is a separate world that they occupy for many hours a day, and they are doing it with or without their parents' blessing. One teenage girl I interviewed says, "My parents made me tell them my [e-mail] password. Then I got a Yahoo! account and they called Yahoo! to get the password. And now I have a new e-mail account that they don't know about." Another said that she is adept at switching screens when she hears a parent approaching. "I'm really fast," she says. "I hear them coming down the stairs and woop! It's gone." Adolescents feel an increasing need to be part of the online world because if they are not, they miss out on a lot of gossip. They also do not understand the language that is born on the Internet but makes its way into the real world: abbreviations such as *brb* (be right back), *lol* (laugh out loud), or code language such as *emo* (for sad, emotional) and *slashy"* (referring to moments when people transgress social norms of sex, gender, or power). Young people who do not understand the code words of their peers quickly feel socially alienated. "Not being on [the social networking site] is like not being at school for a couple of days and missing out on lunch," explains one teenager. "You'll be kind of out of the loop. I think there's a lot of people who do it because they need to be in the loop."

Why does the Internet qualify as its own social context, rather than a subset of an existing one? Most important, it qualifies as its own context because it is qualitatively different from the others and is an important part of identity formation for young people that is not being mediated by adults. It offers independence, playfulness, seriousness, a peer audience. It is a place of intense and unrestricted learning. It has its own etiquette, system of rules, and morality, and it is in constant evolution. In a single generation, there has been a paradigm shift: adolescents inhabit a social context that their parents for the most part did not experience as teenagers. It is a world that many parents still do not really understand. And its ramifications are complex.

Implications for morality and moral development

Is the existence of this new digital social context good or bad? The answer to that question depends on how one thinks about morality. Is morality, as many theorists argue, taught by adults to children? Is it emotionally based and habit driven? And is it strongly associated with acceptance of long-standing traditions of society?[20] If so, the Internet and its social possibilities are dangerous because its rules do not reinforce morality. Or is morality something that is developed by children as they experience life, question their experiences and what they are taught, resolve conflict, and construct meaning about what is right, fair, and good, which does not necessarily entail accepting traditional values as moral? If it is, the Internet is a boon because it encourages questions and provides infinite scenarios in which young people can test their emerging sense of right and wrong. Today, both theorists and laypeople are deeply divided about the essential provenance of morality. The Internet is enormous, anarchic, and anonymous. It is the essential question with no right answers. And so it is fundamentally subversive to some and delightfully empowering to others.

A brief review of the debate over the origin of morality assists us in situating the discourse over electronic social networking in the larger discussion of child moral development. For our purposes, the literature can be divided into two camps. In the first camp, theorists, educators, and parents essentially say that too much freedom, too much questioning is dangerous for adolescents—and for society. In the other camp, theorists, educators, and parents say that freedom and questioning are essential parts of moral formation. Elliot Turiel summarizes this bifurcation in *The Culture of Morality* (2002).

In the first camp, Turiel explains, morality is tied to a particular idea about community, and the fear is that community has declined in recent decades. In this view, he explains, "there is a great and urgent need for renewal by reverting to a greater [traditional] sense of community." There is a sense that society has fostered a "skepticism about morality, along with an emphasis on individual autonomy, personal choice, rights and judgments," and that this "has undermined habitually derived and emotionally based commitments to a community life of interdependence and resulted in increased crime, drug abuse, sexual freedom, and an erosion of families." The prescription is to "return to earlier ways when society was in a better moral state." Turiel explains that these ideas are presented in one form or another by theoreticians generally associated with conservatives, such as William Bennett, Allan Bloom, S. B. Whitehead, and James Dobson, as well as by writers and thinkers often embraced by liberals, such as James Q. Wilson, Robert Bellah, and Amitai Etzioni.[21]

Morality is also tied to character traits of individuals for thinkers in this first camp, as articulated by Emile Durkheim in the early twentieth century and Amitai Etzioni in more recent years. As communitarians see it, individual morality "is attained through emotionally-based, symbolically driven attachment to and respect for, the social order. Two central elements are attachment to society and a 'spirit of discipline.'" Character formation entails the acquisition of core values, transmitted from one generation to the next, that allow people to control impulses and defer gratification. In most of these conceptions, "both the source and ends of morality are in community, society, or culture," and unbridled pursuit of self-interest is bad. The bottom line is that society used to be more harmonious than it is now, and the greater degree of questioning of social and political institutions and cultural traditions represents a decay in community and morality. In short, these writers on both the left and the right "presuppose . . . that the acquisition of morality entails acceptance of, and identification with, the long-standing values, standards, and traditions of the society, and that within cultures standards and values are generally shared."[22] To them the phenomenon of adolescents' free roaming of the Internet presents far more dangers than benefits and thus is deeply problematic.

The second theoretical camp avoids assuming that traditions, such as traditional definitions of community, are by definition good, or that shifting behaviors, even social conflict, necessarily denote a weakening of the social fabric. In this way, the second camp, with its developmental view, is less nostalgic than the communitarian one, which presupposes harmony in traditional systems of societal morality. It is more optimistic and less teleological than the first camp. In this second view, championed by Turiel, there has been no de facto social or moral decline in American society in the last forty years. Instead, Turiel argues, societies are always complex, and conflict is always part of society. It is in resolving conflict that social development takes place. Thus, for example, the apparent social harmony in the mid-twentieth-century United States masked difference in power and the oppression of certain groups. In fact, Turiel asserts, social conflict initiated by powerless groups in society can be a sign of health in the culture. He uses examples of political and social protest movements of the 1950s and 1960s, movements that resulted in a more just society, to make his point:

In the 1960s there was more conflict and open mistrust over racial issues than during the previous decade. It can be asked if the conflict and mistrust reflects deterioration or progress.

Martin Luther King, Jr. of course, did not regard the conflicts as indicative of social deterioration or moral decay. Nor would he have measured the moral state of society by the numbers of people engaged in social institutions. . . . His assessment of the impact of the church on morality and society was based not on the numbers of people participating in its activities, but in the stands its leaders and members *failed* to take regarding matters of justice. He faulted the church for its acceptance of societal arrangements perpetuating racial discrimination. [In fact,] it appears that King thought that participation in group activities and trust in the social system often occur when those groups or social institutions, like the church, help perpetuate long-standing social injustices [emphasis added].[23]

The second camp's theoretical perspective, building on that of Piaget, Kohlberg, and others, views morality as "entailing judgments, [and being] based on the proposition that children construct ways of thinking about welfare, justice and rights through a variety of social experiences." Moral development is not merely a process of adaptation to the social system, and as a result, "existing or past social practices are not necessarily the sources of the moral." In other words, as children develop their moral compass, they learn to analyze their own culture, "and can stand apart from it, scrutinizing societal arrangements and cultural practices."[24] It is precisely because people must weigh and coordinate different domains, some moral, some social, that they can both be a part of their culture and analyze it from the outside. And it is precisely because there is always social conflict revolving around power and norms that force the renegotiation of societal morals that people do not always respond in the same way to conventional morality. Turiel and his colleagues' concepts of social and moral domains of thought are useful in helping us to think about the new social context created by the Internet. We can think of the Internet as a social context that both frees young people from adult control and forces them into conflict and disequilibrium as they interact with others online. It is out of that disequilibrium that moral development takes place. The online world creates its own social context and forces young people to coordinate it with traditional social contexts and their emerging sense of morality.

Evidence suggests that in many ways, Internet-connected teenagers are performing better and are less rebellious than many adults fear. Teenagers' lives are actually still very rule driven. As Steven Johnson has pointed out in *Everything Bad Is Good for You* (as cited by Gladwell), they perform at a higher standard than in years past, and their IQs are higher. They also do tougher math, science, and language work.[25] And as David Brooks observed in "The Organization Kid," they are more scheduled than ever before and rebel against the strictures of society less.[26] But their Internet experience is an area where they are able to be freer than in most other arenas of their lives. And because the rules are not preordained—the beauty of the Internet is its anarchic, anonymous, constantly shifting nature—young people can experiment, explore, and make their own judgments in ways that prove meaningful to them. Internet morality does not seem to replace the morality of adolescents' parents. Rather, it is a way for young people to test hypotheses and experiment with alter egos. Often they make mistakes. But they say it is important for teenagers to be able to make mistakes. "I had a gross interaction with a fifty-seven-year-old man in a chatroom," said one seventeen-year-old girl, "so I changed my e-mail and my screen name and I didn't do that anymore."

Conclusion: There has been a paradigm shift

Adult masters used to hold the key to knowledge and bestow it on the young. Moral traditions were transmitted in the same way. There were bodies of moral teachings to be relayed to the next generation, no questions asked. The world is different today. The information available to young people by way of the

Internet is infinite and cannot be effectively controlled by adults. Learning, in both the academic and the moral sense, is less and less about mastering a finite body of material and more and more about developing the ability to manage too much information: to discern good quality from poor quality, to manage information overload. Communities are more permeable, fragmented, and far flung. Moral development is less about mastering clear right and wrong answers and more about negotiating different social contexts. What young people do after hours, through the windows of their computer screens, has become an important part of their individual and social identity formation and of their moral development.

Notes

1. The characters drawn in this chapter are composite portraits of teenagers taken from interviews conducted by the author. None of the names are real. The quotations are verbatim. All material from the interviews is used with permission from the interviewees.

2. Murray, M. E. (1983). *Moral development and moral education: An overview. Studies in moral development and education: Developing fairness and concern for others.* Retrieved April 15, 2005, from http://tigger.uic.edu/~lnucci/MoralEd/overviewtext.html.

3. Turiel, E. (1983) *The development of social knowledge: Morality and convention.* Cambridge: Cambridge University Press.

4. Murray. (1983).

5. Turiel. (1983, pp. 3, 36).

6. Turiel. (1983, p. 187).

7. Murray, E. (1983).

8. Madden, M. (2003). *America's online pursuits: The changing picture of who's online and what they do.* Pew Internet and American Life Project. Retrieved May 23, 2005, from http://www.pewinternet.org.

9. In fact, LiveJournal, Facebook, and MySpace have recently been sold. MySpace is now worth nearly $600 million, and its new parent company, Intermix Media, is part of the Murdoch media empire and has been accused by New York's attorney general, Elliott Spitzer, of installing spyware and adware on millions of users' machines without giving them proper notice. Caney, D. (2005, July 19). News corp to buy myspace.com owner for $580 million. *Yahoo!News.* Retrieved July 29, 2005, from http://news.yahoo.com/news?tmpl=story&u=/nm/20050719/media_nm/newscorp_dc; Lapinski, T. (2005, July 19). Fox to buy Intermix Media/Myspace: The truth about Myspace. *Apple-x.net.* Retrieved July 29, 2005, from http://apple-x.net/modules.php?op=modload&name=News&file=article&sid=1510.

10. Helem, L. (2001, June 21). Study of teens on Web notes rise of "instant message generation." *Atlanta Journal-Constitution*. Retrieved on August 2, 2005, from ProQuest Newspapers Database.

11. Ma, O. (2003, Jan. 4). Instant messenger addict? *Current Magazine*. Retrieved July 6, 2005, from http://hcs.harvard.edu/~hcurrent/articles/10022/1.html.

12. Turiel. (1983).

13. Sullivan, B. (2005). Kids, blogs and too much information. *MSNBC.com*. Retrieved July 18, 2005, from http://www.msnbc.msn.com/id/7668788/print/1/displaymode/1098/.

14. Sullivan. (2005, Apr. 29).

15. Huffaker, D. (2004). *Gender similarities and differences in online identity and language use among teenage bloggers.* Unpublished doctoral dissertation, Georgetown University; Gardner, S. (2005). Popular Web site makes teens targets. [Douglas County, Georgia] *Record-Courier*. Retrieved July 18, 2005, from http://www.recordcourier.com/apps/pbcs.dll/article?AID=/20050622/News/106220009/0/FRONTPAGE&template=printart; MacDonald, J. (2005). Teens: It's a diary. Adults: It's unsafe. *Christian Science Monitor*. Retrieved May 25, 2005, from http://www.csmonitor.com/2005/0525/p11s02-lifp.html.

16. Huffaker. (2004).

17. Denizet-Lewis, B. (2004, May 30). Friends, friends with benefits and the benefits of the local mall. *New York Times Online Edition*. Retrieved September 14, 2005, from http://select.nytimes.com/search/restricted/article?res=F60713FA3C5A0C738FDDAC0894DC404482.

18. Helem. (2001, June 21).

19. Henning, J. (2005, May 5). Ump teen. Perseus Development Corporation. Retrieved July 29, 2005, from http://www.perseus.com/blogsurvey/blog/050505umpteen.html.

20. Turiel. (2002).

21. Turiel. (2002); Lakoff, G. (2004). *Don't think of an elephant! Know your values and frame the debate*. White River Junction, VT: Chelsea Green Publishing.

22. Turiel. (2002).

23. Turiel. (2002).

24. Turiel. (2002).

25. Gladwell, M. (2005, May 16). Brain candy: Is pop culture dumbing us down or smartening us up? *New Yorker*, 88–89.

26. Brooks, D. (2001, Apr.). The organization kid. *Atlantic Monthly*. Retrieved July 20, 2005, from ProQuest Newspapers and Magazines Database.

KAREN BRADLEY *is the department chair of history and a technology assistant to the faculty at the Head-Royce School, Oakland, California.*

Drawing from empirical research and his own parenting experiences, the author challenges program leaders to go beyond the practice of treating children with disabilities "as if they were normal."

5

Toward ethical approaches to the inclusion of peers with disabilities

Dale Borman Fink

HOW DO SCHOOL-AGED and adolescent youngsters without disabilities think about and act toward their peers who have disabilities, chronic health conditions, or other developmental or behavioral differences? And what would it mean for program operators, coaches, volunteer leaders, and after-school caregivers to help shape their thinking in a direction that we could regard as ethically sound? In this chapter, I propose that leaders should overcome their tendency to avoid speaking openly about disabilities and instead seek out naturally occurring opportunities to do so.

How troop members responded to "disability awareness"

During the research for my book *Making a Place for Kids with Disabilities*, I spent time as a participant-observer in several out-of-school venues that included children with disabilities.[1] Because the Girl Scouts in the small town in central Illinois where I was conducting my research were more receptive than most other

NEW DIRECTIONS FOR YOUTH DEVELOPMENT, NO. 108, WINTER 2005 © WILEY PERIODICALS, INC.

organizations to the participation of children with a variety of special needs, Brownie and Junior Girl Scout troops were among the settings where I regularly recorded my observations. An episode I never previously wrote about involved the presentation of a "disability awareness" puppet troop performance at one of the Brownie troop meetings, followed by an exercise in which the girls "tried on" various kinds of disabilities by using blindfolds, headphones, and having their fingers wrapped together to reduce manual dexterity.

The presentation included puppets with several kinds of physical and sensory disabilities, and the hands-on exercise expanded the range of disabling conditions they could explore. Afterward there was a discussion, giving the seven- and eight-year-old girls—nearly all Caucasian from blue-collar families—a chance to share their feelings, ask questions, and make statements. They did not have many questions, but they expressed a range of empathetic thoughts and feelings. The speaker asked them if they "would be sad if other kids didn't want to play with you because you did things differently." The first hand that shot up was that of Sarah, who was not usually especially talkative: "I would be *mad*," she said, her clear eyes ready to take on anyone who dared differ.

As they wrapped up the discussion, one of the leaders asked these highly engaged youngsters if they knew anyone like the children represented by the puppets or in the exercise. They all shook their heads, agreeing that they did not. This was very instructive, considering that LaToya, one of the members of their troop (who was absent that day), always used a wheelchair, communicated only with a synthesized speech device that she operated with her chin, and needed help from an adult (usually her mother or father) in order to work on any projects that required using her hands.[2] Apparently neither LaToya's differences in self-presentation, her need for support, nor her paraphernalia placed her into the box called "disability" as these girls constructed it in their minds from the puppet performance and the exercises. They still thought of her primarily as "peer" or "member of the troop" rather than a member of this other category that the adults were trying to teach them about.

In that moment of silence, in which the children were nodding their heads innocently to left and right, it must have dawned on the adult leaders that on some level, they had not gotten their lesson across. Yet we might be tempted to clap our hands. Why not rejoice that these young girls were looking past the disabilities, the adult supports, and the equipment to see LaToya first and foremost as a girl and a Brownie like themselves—and perhaps even a potential friend? Wasn't that a wonderful testament to the naturally inclusive spirit of children?

I did take joy in the troop members' disinclination to place a label on LaToya that would separate her from them and also in the way little Sarah's heart was inflamed against the injustice of exclusion. But my joy, while real, had to be only momentary because I knew more about the story—not only LaToya's story but the stories of others who grow beyond the age of Brownies and find their peers no longer living up to that inclusive spirit that animated them in their younger days. I knew, for instance, that the typically develop-ing children, while refraining from putting a label on LaToya, also did not really show an interest in playing with her, sitting next to her, or becoming her friend. Later in this chapter, I return to focus on this same Brownie troop and illustrate how these volunteer lead-ers went beyond this single attempt to infuse disability awareness. But first, I want underscore the insight that this one episode yields.

The silent treatment

It is commonplace in my personal experience and research that staff, instructors, coaches, and caregivers in a wide variety of out-of-school activities avoid direct discussion or acknowledgment of the disabilities of children in their groups, in the mistaken belief that this is the best way to demonstrate that all children are equal and to avoid the perception of discrimination. Disabilities—even when they are readily apparent—are treated as if they were invisible.

Discussions with individual children and families about their conditions and needs are kept private. Disabilities as a general topic may
on occasion be considered a proper subject for discussion (as with
the "disability-awareness" activities), but the differing needs, supports, or developmental issues of individual participants are not. If
other children do not witness their leaders and caregivers (and family members) communicating openly about these subjects, then they
get the message that disabilities should be shrouded in silence.

Jennifer, who was deaf, was an active member of a Junior Girl Scout
troop (ages nine to eleven). The school district sent her to a nearby
city for schooling, so unlike the other troop members, she did not
know any of them from school; the troop was her best opportunity for
social interaction with girls from her own neighborhood. Her mother
was the assistant volunteer troop leader and acted as a sign language
interpreter for some portions of the meetings. Gretchen, the troop
leader, had known the family since their children were born and told
me that Jennifer was a "bright child" who could do anything the other
girls could do and did not need any special supports other than the
sign language interpreting. I learned that her idea of "no special supports" extended even to the introduction of new girls into the troop:

I was present when several new girls joined Jennifer's Junior Girl Scout
troop. When it was Jennifer's turn, she made some whispered sounds,
which were not easily intelligible. Translating for her, Gretchen said,
"This is Jennifer." No one, then or subsequently, pointed out to the new
girls that Jennifer was deaf or suggested ways of communicating with her,
such as learning some signs, making gestures, or writing . . . on a note pad.[3]

I am sure that each new girl eventually figured out that Jennifer
was deaf. But the fact that the leaders never stated it conveyed the
message that talking openly about Jennifer's deafness and how to
work around it was off-limits. Yet without such a discussion, girls
could not include Jennifer as they talked with one another, and
there was little chance anyone would become friends with her.
Moreover, as preadolescents, these girls had a heightened con-
sciousness about any and all differences in development and appear-

ance. I heard them speaking to each other about who had gotten eyeglasses, braces, retainers, and expanders. Jennifer's differences must have intrigued them, but without permission or encouragement to focus on it, they kept any questions to themselves.

In another Brownie troop, the leaders not only remained silent in front of the troop members about Arianna's disability (she used a wheelchair), but it also took them several weeks before they even had a conversation with the parents about how Arianna would go to the toilet and what kinds of support she would need there. Luckily, they had that conversation before the day arrived that Arianna did have to use the facilities. But their reluctance to initiate such a conversation is a reflection of the widespread (and, in my opinion, ill-conceived) ethos that states that it is bad form to openly acknowledge developmental differences and disabilities.

This pattern I am describing is not a result of inattention or thoughtlessness. I am speaking of leaders and caregivers who have thought about it and who believe they are doing the right thing— the ethical thing—by avoiding acknowledgment of individual differences.

"At the Boys and Girls Club," for example, "a member of the staff described how he would reply to questions from other youth about Artie's way of speaking or behaving: 'He has a disability, and we would appreciate if you would look over that, and treat him as a normal person.'"[4]

Overcoming barriers to social interaction

There are many children who need no special help to communicate, play, and make friends during out-of-school activities, even though they do need extra support in the academic environment. I do not suggest that a discussion with peers is required or desirable in connection with every child who has a disability and participates in a recreation center, dance or music studio, camp, troop, team, or after-school program. But I do suggest that when a child's disability or condition is likely to make it harder for her or him to become fully included in a peer group, the ethical approach is for leaders to initiate communication in order to enable the peers to have the tools and understanding with which to act in an inclusive manner. This is not to imply that all the peers will take such guidance to heart. But within any given team, troop, or after-school group, there may be one or two who will respond to this kind of guidance. Any parent of a child with a disability can vouch for the fact that one peer who relates in a meaningful way to their child is infinitely greater than zero.

Parental permission to share information with peers

The discussion with peers should not focus on such private matters as the participant's diagnosis, medical history, or current medications. It should focus on the issues germane to playing, working, learning, and communicating together: what kinds of support to offer (or not to offer), what modes of communication to use, how to respond to unwanted behavior, what to do in the event of a medical episode. Wouldn't it be more ethical to coach children on how to respond to a child with Down syndrome who hugs excessively rather than say nothing and stand by as they begin to avoid the child? Wouldn't it be more ethical to teach peers to recognize when a child is going into insulin shock rather than keep them in the dark about her diabetes? Wouldn't it be more ethical to teach all children how to say their names in sign language, so that the next time they go around the table introducing themselves, the one child who is deaf will not feel so isolated? Wouldn't it be more ethical for leaders to explain to peers that a child's attention deficit makes it hard for him to concentrate and follow directions at certain times, and model for them some creative ways of offering alternatives rather than modeling the already well-worn punitive response?

Of course, the parent or guardian has to authorize any sharing of personal information about a child's disabilities with members of the peer group. Even if the focus is mostly on strategies for interacting with the child, parental permission has to be requested and received. Depending on the organization and the situation, it might be formal and written or informal. No matter what the circumstances and no matter how formal or informal the parental consent process, a conversation with the family should always precede any discussion with members of the peer group. In connection with getting permission to go forward, the leader and the parent should come to some general understanding as to what information will be shared and what advice will be provided.

Beyond "disability awareness" to learning in context

The volunteer leaders who arranged for the disability puppet performance recognized that their Brownie members were not able to draw meaningful connections from the presentation to their own peer, LaToya. Some weeks later, they tried a different approach. They arranged for the troop to meet at LaToya's house and experience, up close and personal, the ways in which LaToya received support for eating, bathing, learning, communicating, and mobility. Among other hands-on activities, each girl took a turn getting raised and lowered into a bathtub (fully clothed and with no water in the tub) by means of a mechanical device that the family used for LaToya. This was a much more successful approach to raising awareness and the capacity for building relationships. At least one girl who had previously been frightened of going near LaToya now took a much greater interest in her (as the girl's mother explained to me).

I believe this approach—building on naturally occurring opportunities to learn about individual needs and supports—can lead us toward ethical practices in supporting typically developing youth to communicate, play, learn, and work better with their peers who have disabilities. When there is a meaningful context such as personal acquaintance, peers are primed to learn a great deal and to have a positive attitude. It is then up to the leaders to find the right way, within the parameters of their own mission, schedule, and resources, to create opportunities for this kind of context-based learning. What the Girl Scout leaders did was a perfect illustration of that.

What I am proposing will fly in the face of some people's humanistic impulses. I am asking program leaders to stop putting out the message that "in spite of our differences, we are all normal." I am suggesting that they broadcast a very different message. First, drop the concept of normalcy; it serves no function. The point is that we all are members of the team, the club, the troop, the community. We all belong together.

Second, there are among us individuals who learn, communicate, play, move about, and behave in a variety of ways. When any of those differences creates a barrier, it is the job of the rest of us—youth and adults—to figure out how to get across the barrier. In fact, each of us may find at some point in our life that our own differences separate us from our peers and threaten our sense of belonging. It may be due to a disability, a problem in our family, or any number of other reasons. We will be grateful when our peers look for ways to overcome those barriers and help us to feel that we still belong.

The younger children are, the more they resist putting their peers into the boxes that come so easily later on, and the more completely open they are to the kinds of messages I am proposing. When they reach adolescence, some of the typically developing youth will inevitably turn away from their peers with disabilities, lacking the strength or the self-esteem to associate themselves with those whose appearance, behavior, or learning styles may be not be considered "cool." But I believe the proportion of teens (and adults too) who maintain a positive connection to their peers with disabilities will be greater if we have exposed them as early as possible to meaningful strategies to bridge the gaps with their peers rather than teaching them a bland form of acceptance in which "everyone is normal."

Context-based learning about disability in my own family

As this volume goes to press, my son is turning five. Let's call him Jeremy. He does not know about the category of "disability." He has learned through personal encounters or storybooks, however, about a variety of ways people have of doing things, according to their needs and abilities. Albert, whom we regularly see in synagogue, uses a wheelchair. My son does not see him as helpless or unfortunate: prior to the rabbi's reading from the Torah (the Hebrew scroll containing the first five books of the Bible), Albert is often selected to come forward and recite the very important blessings. After the service, he is the first person Jeremy crosses the sanctuary to greet.

Another member of our congregation walked with a cane for several months and needed to use the elevator to go between the sanctuary and the reception room. Later, she gave up the cane, but Jeremy learned that she still preferred the elevator rather than walking the stairs. Even at his young age, Jeremy can recognize that the interactions between one's level of impairment and one's needs for support or accommodation are endlessly variable.

Jeremy finds the paraphernalia that accompanies some disabilities fascinating and sometimes makes lists in his mind—for example, of all the different devices that help people to walk. "There's wheelchairs, walkers, crutches, canes. Dad, is there any other things that help people walk?"

Both of Jeremy's grandfathers wear hearing aids, and he loves pretending that he has them as well. Due to his pediatrician's having a day off one day last year, we had to bring Jeremy to a colleague of hers for a checkup. Just as she got ready to shine a light in his ears, Jeremy startled her by saying, "Oh, excuse me. I have to take out my hearing aid."

Our family passed an empty wheelchair at the edge of a beach parking lot last summer. Jeremy expressed astonishment: if someone needed a wheelchair to get this far, how could he or she give it up at the beach? Soon his curiosity and mine were satisfied, as we saw a man pushing another man in a wheelchair with inflatable tires, reminiscent of bicycle tires designed for beach riding. We strolled to the edge of the water and engaged the two of them in conversation and learned they parked the other chair and transferred to this one, which they called his "beach buggy."

Jeremy asked me after our last visit to my home town in the Midwest if his aunt Laurel, my sister, came from a different country, because the way she talked was "sort of like an accent." I lauded him for being such a good listener and observer but explained that she did not come from a different country. I did not teach him the term *Down syndrome* yet, but explained that ever since she was a baby, Aunt Laurel learned things more slowly and sometimes differently and that her speech sounded different from me and from his other aunts and uncles because of that.

In *Drummer Hoff*, one of Jeremy's preferred stories for years, the characters are a succession of soldiers of progressively higher rank.[5] Although readers would know this only from the art and not the text, Sergeant Chowder walks with a prosthesis beginning at his left knee and Captain Bammer wears a patch over his right eye. Both, I explained when my son was three years old, were casualties of war. Yet each still continued to do important work: Sergeant Chowder brought the powder, and Captain Bammer brought the rammer.

As I was completing writing this chapter, Jeremy informed me with some confidence that the man who was fixing his training wheel bike in a local shop (let's call him Douglas) used to be a soldier. He figured this out, he told me, because the man has a hook in place of one hand. I told him that I was not sure if Douglas had lost his hand in a war, but it was possible. I explained that sometimes people's bodies grow and develop in different ways, even from the time they are babies, and also that people sometimes lose a hand in an accident rather than a war. I also told him the correct name for the "hook" was a *prosthesis* but said it was fine if he wanted to call it a hook. But the most important thing I told him was that next time we are in the shop together, I will ask Douglas at what age or by what means he acquired the current configuration of his hand. Unless we are brave enough to have honest and respectful conversations with individuals with disabilities whom we encounter within the contexts of our own lives, how can we make any claims about guiding youth toward ethical practices in this arena?

Notes

1. Fink, D. B. (2000). *Making a place for kids with disabilities.* Westport, CT: Greenwood Press.

2. I am using the same fictional names for children mentioned in this chapter as in the book. Fink. (2000).

3. Fink. (2000). Pp. 182–183.

4. Fink. (2000). P. 177.

5. Emberly, E. R., & Emberly, B. (1967). *Drummer Hoff.* New York: Simon & Schuster.

DALE BORMAN FINK *is an independent scholar based in Williamstown, Massachusetts. He also holds a faculty appointment at the University of Connecticut Center for Excellence in Developmental Disabilities.*

*A researcher handed disposable cameras to a group
of urban youth, active members of a Boys and Girls
Club. They used the snapshots they took to tell her
about their positive social connections to peers and
adults and explain how the environment of the club
had nurtured those connections.*

6

"I like to treat others as others would treat me": The development of prosocial selves in an urban youth organization

Nancy L. Deutsch

THE FIELD OF MORAL development has moved toward an identity-based model suggesting that moral action stems not only from moral reasoning but from a desire to act in ways consistent with one's self-concept. Moral identity, in turn, is rooted in social relationships.[1] This idea, that our sense of self drives moral behavior and that this identity is constructed through connections to others, influences the ways in which we envision adolescent development and how we nurture morality and ethics in teens. The notion that moral identity is embedded in our relationships has both practical

I thank the youth and staff at the East Side Boys and Girls Club for sharing their lives and Barton J. Hirsch for his comments on prior versions of this chapter.

NEW DIRECTIONS FOR YOUTH DEVELOPMENT, NO. 108, WINTER 2005 © WILEY PERIODICALS, INC.

and theoretical implications for the field of youth development and for how we design settings for adolescents.

This chapter is drawn from an in-depth study of an urban youth organization. The most dramatic finding is the high level of prosocial traits, especially respect, that youth report as integral to their identities. For many, these traits are tied to their experiences at the center and the relationships they build there. Their narratives describe a process of transformation and self-construction reminiscent of the literature on moral identity. We must pay attention to this phenomenon and seek to understand the contextual and relational factors that enhance the development of prosocial identities in adolescents. Youth organizations, if designed appropriately, may provide a setting for social interactions and relationships in which youth can enact and receive validation for moral behaviors and develop prosocial selves.

The prosocial self: Ethics, relationships and identity

When we talk about adolescent identity, we often focus on separation. It is true that teens individuate from their families and stake out an autonomous sense of self.[2] Yet this separation is not a severing of ties. Adolescents need relationships with supportive adults. Relationships have an impact on youths' experiences in schools and after-school programs, psychosocial health, academic outcomes, and identity, including moral and civic identities.[3] Autonomy can exist within a community of support; individual goals and responsibility toward others need not be seen as conflicting.[4] Relationships provide teens with a safe base for identity exploration and a sense of fulfillment that is critical to psychological health.[5] Adolescents develop relational skills through "practice" relationships and need a network of people on whom to rely for social capital as they enter adulthood.[6] Opportunities for bonding with peers and adults, building supportive relationships, and practicing prosocial norms are important features of positive developmental settings.[7] The true conflict of adolescence may in fact revolve around connection, not separation.[8]

Affective ties to others are also important for nurturing moral-ity. It is through social relationships that moral goals and identities are shaped.[9] Forming relationships with and feeling connected to others is also important.[10] Within relationships, adolescents can "try on" and receive validation for moral identities.[11] Such moral identity is crucial to moral action. It is not moral reasoning and judgment alone that lead to behavior but the unity of self and moral goals.[12] For adolescents, prosocial and moral identities may evolve in part through community service experiences.[13]

Research has begun to examine after-school programs as sites of social integration that promote prosocial norms.[14] Yet less is known about how comprehensive youth organizations, which incorporate some elements of community service and social responsibility but are not focused around these goals, foster changes in adolescents' identities that may drive moral behavior. The literature suggests that supportive social relationships in after-school settings can help youth construct prosocial selves, but the mechanisms behind this are not clear.

This study

The data presented here are drawn from a project examining a Boys and Girls Club as a site for identity development. I chose qualitative methods because of my interest in the process of ado-lescent development in a natural setting.[15] I combined four years of participant-observation with focus groups, semistructured inter-views, and photography projects to examine how the program func-tions as a developmental space.

Method

The East Side Boys and Girls Club sits on the outskirts of a hous-ing project in a large midwestern city.[16] The building is small but has a variety of activity areas. The hallways are filled with laughter and scampering feet. There are occasional conflicts, bored kids, and burned-out staff, yet the overall atmosphere is energetic. There are scheduled team practices and group meetings, but youth are otherwise free to choose their activities. Staff oversee the entrance and ask youth to sign in and hang up their jackets as they enter. There are behavior and dress codes, which are enforced by staff and youth alike, but interactions overall are informal and casual.

The ethnographic sample includes all youth and staff present at East Side over the four years. I conducted interviews and photography projects with seventeen youth ages twelve to eighteen (nine females). Seven were between the ages of twelve and fourteen, and ten were fifteen or older at the time of their first interview. Ten youth describe their race or ethnicity as black or African American, two as African American and Hispanic, two as African American plus two additional ethnicities, and one each as Hispanic, white, or other. Fourteen youth live in the housing project near the club. The remaining three have close ties to it. All seventeen are active members who have been coming to the club for a number of years or come to the club on a regular basis.

I did not randomly select participants. I was interested in how the Boys and Girls Club is used as a setting for identity work, so it was important to have youth who were actively involved. I attempted to recruit youth I did not know through staff recommendations but had an easier time enlisting youth whom I already knew. This may bias the sample. Yet it may also enhance my findings, as I had trusting relationships established with many of the participants.

Measures

I conducted four years of participant-observation at East Side. Five research assistants also did fieldwork during that time. Many youth were present over all four years, making it possible to look at how youth participated in the club over time. In the third year, I conducted two focus groups: one with club members ages twelve to fourteen and one with members age fifteen and older. In the fourth year, I conducted two, one-on-one, semistructured interviews with seventeen youth. Each interview lasted forty-five to sixty minutes. Youth were given gift certificates as compensation. All seventeen youth completed the first interview; fourteen completed the second interview. Topics included youths' sense of self, club experiences, and race, class, and gender issues. I also gave each youth a disposable camera and asked them to photograph things such as an adult to whom they are close, something that represents their future goals, and their favorite things in the club. Half the film could be used for pictures of anything they felt would tell me more about who they are. The second interview drew on the photos for its content.

Analysis

The analytic process was iterative. I wrote field and analytical notes after each site visit. I examined my notes for emerging themes and used these to inform future observations and interviews.[17] Interview topics were developed from the focus group data and the identity literature. I developed codes to represent the theoretical themes in the data. Some codes came from the identity literature (e.g., connected vs. individuated self-concept) and some came from the youth themselves (e.g., respect and responsibility). I analyzed the interviews for these codes.[18] The connected and individuated self codes were checked with a second rater for reliability.[19] I then returned to the field notes and coded them, using a modified form of constant comparison to shift between data sources, identifying themes and the links between them.[20] As themes emerged I explored them through my field work and interviews. One of the emergent codes, respect, is the focus of this paper. This construct was striking in the abundance with which it appeared across data sources and subjects.

My findings are clearly limited by the fact that I rely on self-report data. I did not, for example, ask youths' parents or teachers to describe them to see if the teens' images of themselves as respectful individuals transferred to others' views of them or to other settings. However, the four years of observations, combined with my conversations with staff and parents at the club, provide limited triangulation of my findings. Some staff and parents reported seeing youth evolve prosocially as they became more involved in the club. Of course, we might expect that many of us would want to see and describe ourselves to outsiders as respectful. The youths' self-reports alone therefore must be considered within the context of their actions as I observed them over the years. I cannot say whether or how these actions transferred to other contexts or people in their lives.

Results and discussion

This study did not start out as being about prosocial or moral identities. Rather, I set out to examine a youth organization as a site for self-construction overall. Yet as I analyzed the data, I found that the process of identity development at East Side supports the construction of identities that are in rich connection to other people and encourage prosocial characteristics. The club serves as a distinct setting for relational and autonomous self-construction. Respect emerges consistently in the narratives of youth. Not only do they use this word to describe themselves, but their stories of self-construction often revolve around related themes. Narratives of respect frequently involve East Side as a setting in which it is developed and nurtured. Observations confirm this, showing many instances in which staff and youths' interactions embody respect. The use of respect to describe the self, and the active way in which it is nurtured through social interaction, is linked to the development of moral identities as described in the literature.

Youths' self-descriptions

In the first interview, I asked youth for the five words that describe them the best. I coded these self-descriptors into two categories: connected and individual. Connected words refer to youths' relationships with others. Individual words describe a trait that is independent of connections with other people.[21] All but one youth used at least one connected word among their five self-descriptors. Four youth used only connected words. The majority of youth, both boys and girls, used them equally. Some examples of participants' five self-descriptors include:

Lover, respectful, fun, happy, smart. Happy and *smart* are the most important. *Lover* means fun to be around, caring. *Respectful* means honest, trustworthy. [Dynasty, fifteen-year-old African American female]

Intelligent, relaxed, clever, responsible, mature. Responsible [is the] most important . . . because I take on everything and I complete the tasks I need to get where I need to be. [Kelly, sixteen-year-old African American male]

Kindness, truthfulness, helpfulness, attitudes. Kindness is most important. I help out with the club when they need help. I tell the truth. . . . I help my momma around the house. . . . [At the club] I be kind to kids. [Moonie, twelve-year-old Hispanic female]

Funny, loud, loving, short, respectful. Respectful is the most important. . . I be funny around people, like me to tell jokes and stuff. . . Loving with my family. . . I give people a lot of respect. I know a lot of stuff. [Greg, twelve-year-old mixed-race male]

Youth are able to balance relational qualities with individual talents to create holistic identities that exist in relationship to, but are not subsumed by, others. Most youth feel that their self-characteristics are encouraged and appreciated at the club, especially the relational qualities. As noted, respect, a prosocial trait, emerged consistently.

I opened the first interview with the question, "Tell me about yourself. Describe yourself to me." Four of the seventeen youth (24 percent) included the word *respectful* in their response. Seven (41 percent) used words such as *caring, responsible, kind,* or *loving.* In their five self-descriptors, six youth (35 percent) included *respectful,* and ten (59 percent) used words such as *nice, helpful, caring, kind,* or *responsible.* Four (24 percent) said *respectful* is their most important quality.

That is not to suggest that youth portray themselves as twenty-four-hour-a-day stand-up citizens. They acknowledged contradictions: "I'm caring. I can be mean sometimes." "I'm nice, respectful, but I have a bad attitude." "I'm kind to people who are kind to me." These selves are contextual. Yet the self is not shifting in relation only to activity or role, but to other people. These are prosocial selves that respect and respond to their relationships with others. This is in line with prior work suggesting that minority teens show heightened awareness of concern for others in their identities.[22] In the coming sections, I examine the meaning of respect and explore how it emerges through youths' words and actions at East Side. I discuss the implications of respect for the field of youth development, especially with regard to nurturing moral identities and prosocial selves.

The meaning of respect

Although contrary to the American middle-class mythology of adolescence, the image of a respectful teen sustains norms valued in African American culture. Respect is part of the legacy of slavery for African Americans, who had to find codes of behavior that showed deference to whites while maintaining self-dignity.[23] Respect has been found to be valued by African American women over and above being liked.[24] Respect is linked to African codes of honor and community. In the African American religious community, there has been a call to reconnect with this "covenant of respect."[25] African American teens have been noted to demand personal respect, which may be associated with a strong sense of right and wrong that permeates notions of self, friendship, and community.[26] Respect is also linked to authority; adolescents are aware that power and respect are connected.[27]

Respect has structural implications. As minority and working-class men have faced displacement from the labor market, traditional masculine routes to respect have been removed. The decline of manufacturing, the movement of jobs to the suburbs, and the increase in service jobs have left many men without the means to achieve respect through work.[28] In such circumstances, alternative paths to respect may be sought. Participation in the underground economy of drugs and violence, hypermasculinity, and consumerism have been suggested as means of seeking respect.[29] Thus, the youths' discourses of respect demand that we address the individual need for respect from a more structural level.

On a personal level, respect is bidirectional. To demonstrate and earn respect, you must be willing to appreciate and listen to others.[30] Respect can be a mutual quality that reflects values of community orientation.[31] Youths' descriptions of respect illustrate this:

I talk more like I'm older but I don't disrespect anybody. Unless they disrespect me. I tell people when I first meet them, just treat me nice, that's all I ask. [Dynasty, fifteen-year-old African American female]

Respectful [is my most important trait]. I like to treat others as others will treat me. [Lorenzo, seventeen-year-old African American male]

I respect staff and so they respect me. [Alyiah, fifteen-year-old African American female]

The staff echoed this bidirectional theme of respect. Charles, the physical education instructor, said, ". . . At first these girls would be gettin' pregnant and stuff. . . . When we have dances or sleep-overs they be trying to sneak over together or what not. . . . But they know not to try anything, because they know what [staff] expect of them and they respect us just like we respect them. But these guys were bad when I first came . . ." As Charles was talking, teen boys were filtering into the room, getting ready for a group meeting. As one boy came into the room talking loudly and trying to get Charles's attention, another boy said, "Be quiet, he talking, man!"

Both youth and staff recognized the importance of symmetry in respectful interaction. Charles's acknowledgment that the boys "were bad" when he was first getting to know them but that they now know what he expects of them and lives up to it illustrates his understanding of the time and energy it takes to earn respect. Charles recognized the teens' requirement that adults treat them as the adults themselves expect to be treated. The boy who was shushing his peer showed that respect in action.

Some youth acknowledged that there are situations in which respect is required regardless of whether it is returned, especially with adults. This type of respect mimics the outward behaviors without the inner affect of respect. This is reflected by youths' statements that they may act in a certain way around adults but do not respect people who do not respect them:

I'm around my teacher, . . . my auntie or somebody, I'm not really bad. Or if I'm around an adult. But when I'm hanging out with my friends I may curse or say mean things, be bad. . . . I have respect for the adults and I don't want to get in trouble if I say something I have no business saying. So I just hold my peace until I'm away from them. But if they don't give me respect then I don't respect them. That's just how I am. [Carla, fourteen-year-old African American female]

This respect is different. Carla does not want "to get in trouble" and hence curbs her behavior. It is not out of mutual respect but fear of consequences. Respect for authority is important, and the ability to understand and respect legitimate authority is an important part of citizenship.[32] This process is enhanced, however, if youth feel respected by the individuals in authority.

The willingness to display respect in response to receiving it is evident in youths' actions surrounding East Side's rules. Codes of behavior and dress are enforced. At times club members admonish each other for breaking these rules. The statement, "we're in the club, man," often punctuates such reprimands, indicating that a respect for the rules is part of respecting the club.

Rick, the club director, feels that the models of respect that youth see in the club help them develop prosocial behaviors themselves. "They get respect in so many ways. [They see it demonstrated] staff to staff, staff to parent, staff don't yell at kids. We say please, we say thank you." Rick sees this rub off on the teenagers in their own behavior toward the club. He acknowledges that they police themselves when it comes to club rules and points to the lack of damage to club property as demonstrating that "kids respect the club and treat it as their own."

When Sean, the program director, began working at East Side, he did not feel that the youth were respectful toward each other or staff. He sees this rooted in a lack of self-respect: "How you gonna respect someone when you don't even respect yourself? That's where it starts, with self-respect." Two years later, Sean reiterated this linkage: "I radiate, and basically with no excuse expect, first and foremost respect for yourself. Don't be looking, acting, talking like an idiot and in return I will give you the respect you deserve."

Staff infuse respect into their interactions with youth by gentle reminders about behavior and through their own modes of relations. Often while I was talking with staff, club members would walk up and interrupt. Each time this occurred, the staff member would look at the youth, acknowledge her presence, and say something like, "You can see that I'm talking with this person. It is disrespectful to interrupt. If you need to speak to me now, you have to say 'excuse me.'" The youth would nod, apologize, and say "excuse me." The staff would say "excuse me" to me and turn to the child: "Okay, now tell me what's up." In doing so, staff members respect youths' needs but also insist on giving respect in order to receive it. Attention, particularly in the form of appreciation and validation of others, is a key aspect of respectful interaction. In interaction with youth, this can come in the form of listening to and validating youths' voices, ideas, and needs.[33] This form of respect is not just lip-service at the club. Respect for the individual youth may be one of the traits of the club that makes it a supportive environment.[34] Respectful relationships can also provide safe spaces in which youth can try on moral identities.[35]

The importance of bidirectional respect has consequences for youth workers. Many adults believe that teenagers should respect them simply because they are adults. But without bidirectional respect, adults are not seen as deserving of respect.[36] Rick notes that assuming respect based on position is a common mistake made by new staff. He and Charles earned respect over many years of working at East Side.

Rick's path to respect involved demonstrating not only that he had respect for the young people but that he held all of them in the same respect and regard. One night an alumnus of the club, a large twenty-year-old man nicknamed Mad Dog, walked into the gym with a friend cursing up a storm. Rick called out to Mad Dog to quit that kind of talk in the club. Mad Dog immediately came over, apologized, and shook Rick's hand. A younger teen boy who was sitting behind Rick reacted with shock. "Man! You get respect from everyone!" the boy said, shaking his head in amazement. The boy was impressed both that Rick had called Mad Dog on his behavior and that Mad Dog had reacted in such a respectful manner. It is this type of consistent respectful behavior from the staff that Rick sees as helping youth to develop a sense of respect. East Side is an environment that models and nurtures prosocial behaviors through expectations and conferring of bidirectional respect.

From hard-headed to respectful: East Side as a site of prosocial transformation

Because most youth have been coming to the club for years, East Side provides a space in which they can connect their past, present, and future selves. Given the prevalence of the ethos of respect, it is not surprising that some members' links between the past and present revolve around this characteristic. The club as a site of transformation from "bad" to "good" kid was fairly common, although more common among the males than the females. Eleven of the seventeen participants said they would not be the same person they are today without the club. In talking about how they would be different if they had not come to the club, many, including twelve-year-old Greg, an African American, said that they would not be as respectful or mature as they are today. Antonio, a fourteen year old of African American and Puerto Rican ethnicity, described himself as "a little terror" when he started coming to the club. If he had not come to the club, he thinks he would "probably be more disrespectful, still running around crazy, still have bad behavior, temper and stuff. . . . When I first met Charles I was kind of disrespectful. As I got to know him he taught me to calm down, control my temper."

Nicole, a fifteen-year-old African American girl, said that when she was younger, she was "bad, hard headed." Now, however, "I'm not a bad child. I might be mean but I'm not a bad child. . . . I don't have time to be bad." Nicole attributed this to her participation in the club. She said that she would not be the same person that she is today if she had not come to the club "because I have a bad attitude. I think my attitude would be worse than it is. I think I wouldn't believe in myself." These stories have a redemptive tinge, describing a transformation from bad to good that comes through their participation at East Side.

Studies of adults' life stories demonstrate a link between a redemption narrative and generativity.[37] Although the qualities described by East Side members, such as respect, responsibility, caring, and kindness, are not generativity in the strict sense of the word, they contain elements of it. Research on morality and citizenship in young adults suggests that these factors may be linked to viewing one's identity as in connection to others and to generativity in middle age.[38] Furthermore, many moral exemplars experience a transformation during which moral goals become central to their sense of self.[39] The process through which the East Side youth travel at the club may be a more everyday version of such self-transformation.

This suggests that a site in which youth participate over time and that provides and expects respect as part of its cultural norms can help youth develop prosocial selves, which in turn may nurture the development of moral and ethical identities. Participation in such organizations can engender civic engagement through modeling moral behavior and learning through practice.[40] These findings indicate that it is not only modeling moral behavior but expecting it that helps youth develop a sense of self built around prosocial characteristics.

Conclusion

What comes through from these narratives of respect is a sense of a connected self embedded in a web of social relations that inform the adolescent's identity. This vision, of a prosocial teen, is not the stereotypical view of adolescence. Yet both boys and girls at East Side describe themselves as rooted in rich relational milieus that provide a context for their developing identities and allow them to define themselves prosocially. The theme of respect is an important part of their self-descriptions. My findings point out the ways in which an environment can support the development of prosocial norms and a connected sense of self and, while doing so, sustain the active participation of adolescents. Such sites may nurture the everyday values that should characterize our lives and foster moral and ethical identities that enhance society.[41]

Notes

1. Blasi, A. (1984). Moral identity: Its role in moral functioning. In W. Kurtines & J. L. Gewirtz (Eds.), *Morality, moral behavior, and moral development* (pp. 128–139). Hoboken, NJ: Wiley; Colby, A. (2002). Moral understanding, motivation, and identity. *Human Development, 45*(2), 130–135; Hart, D., Atkins, R., & Ford, D. (1998). Urban America as a context for the development of moral identity in adolescence. *Journal of Social Issues, 54*(3), 513–530; Hart, D., & Fegley, S. (1995). Prosocial behavior and caring in adolescence: Relations to self-understanding and social judgment. *Child Development, 66*(5), 1346–1359; Reimer, K. (2003). Committed to caring: Transformation in adolescent moral identity. *Applied Developmental Science, 7*(3), 129–137.

2. Steinberg, L. (1990). Autonomy, conflict, and harmony in the family relationship. In S. S. Feldman & G. R. Elliott (Eds.), *At the threshold: The developing adolescent* (pp. 255–276). Cambridge, MA: Harvard University Press.

3. Reimer. (2003); Rhodes, J. E. (2004). The critical ingredient: Caring youth-staff relationships in after-school settings. In G.G. Noam (Ed.), *After-school worlds: Creating a new social space for development and learning* (pp. 145-161). New Directions for Youth Development, no. 101. San Francisco: Jossey-Bass; Saft, E. W., & Pianta, R. C. (2001). Teachers' perceptions of their relationships with students: Effects of child age, gender, and ethnicity of teachers and children. *School Psychology Quarterly, 16*(2), 125–141; Bernstein-Yamashiro, B. (2004). Learning relationships: Teacher-student connections, learning, and identity in high school. In G.G. Noam & N. Fiore (Eds.), *The transforming power of adult-youth relationships* (pp. 55-70). New Directions for Youth Development, no. 103. San Francisco: Jossey-Bass; Noam, G. G. and Fiore, N. (2004). Relationships across multiple settings: An overview. In G.G. Noam & N. Fiore (Eds.), *The transforming power of adult-youth relationships* (pp. 9-16). New Directions for Youth Development, no. 103. San Francisco: Jossey Bass; Roffman, J. G., Pagano, M. E., & Hirsch, B. (2001). Youth functioning and the experiences of inner-city after-school programs among age, gender, and race groups. *Journal of Child and Family Studies, 10*(1), 85–100; Goldsmith, J., Arbreton, A., Arbreton, A. J. A., & Bradshaw, M. (2004). *Promoting emotional and behavioral health in preteens: Benchmarks of success and challenges among programs in Santa Clara and San Mateo counties.* Palo Alto, CA: Lucile Packard

Foundation for Children's Health and Public/Private Ventures; Damon, W. (1998). Political development for a democratic future: A commentary. *Journal of Social Issues*, *54*(3), 621–628; Nasir, N. S., & Kirshner, B. (2003). The cultural construction of moral and civic identities. *Applied Developmental Science*, *7*(3), 138–147.

4. Colby, A., & Damon, W. (1995). The development of extraordinary moral commitment. In M. Killen & D. Hart (Eds.), *Morality in everyday life: Developmental perspectives* (pp. 342–370). Cambridge: Cambridge University Press.

5. Debats, D. L. (1999). Sources of meaning: An investigation of significant commitments in life. *Journal for Humanistic Psychology*, *39*(4), 30–57; Flum, H., & Lavi-Yudelevitch, M. (2002). Adolescents' relatedness and identity formation: A narrative study. *Journal of Social and Personal Relationships*, *19*(4), 527–548.

6. Larson, R., Wilson, S., Brown, B. B., Furstenberg, F. F., & Verma, S. (2002). Changes in adolescents' interpersonal experiences: Are they being prepared for adult relationships in the 21st century? *Journal of Research on Adolescence*, *12*(1), 31–68.

7. Goldsmith et al. (2004); Catalano, R. F., Berglund, M. L., Ryan, J. A., Lonczak, H. S., & Hawkins, J. D. (2002). Positive youth development in the United States: Research findings on evaluations of positive youth development programs. *Prevention and Treatment*, *5*, art. 15.

8. Newman, B. M., & Newman, P. R. (2001). Group identity and alienation: Giving the we its due. *Journal of Youth and Adolescence*, *30*(5), 515–538; Stevens, J. W. (1997). African American female adolescent identity development: A three-dimensional perspective. *Child Welfare*, *76*(1), 145–173.

9. Reimer. (2003); Colby & Damon. (1995); Flanagan, C. (2004). Institutional support for morality: Community-based and neighborhood organizations. In T. A. Thorkildsen & H. J. Walberg (Eds.), *Nurturing morality issues in children's and families' lives* (pp. 173–183). New York: Kluwer Academic/Plenum.

10. Blasi. (1984); Hart et al. (1998); Reimer. (2003).

11. Hart et al. (1998); Colby & Damon. (1995).

12. Blasi. (1984); Colby. (2002); Hart et al. (1998); Hart & Fegley. (1995); Colby & Damon. (1995).

13. Atkins, R., & Hart, D. (2003). Neighborhoods, adults and the development of civic identity in urban youth. *Applied Developmental Science*, *7*(3), 156–164; Hansen, D. M., Larson, R. W., & Dworkin, J. B. (2003). What adolescents learn in organized youth activities: A survey of self-reported developmental experiences. *Journal of Research on Adolescence*, *13*(1), 25–55; Yates, M., & Youniss, J. (1996). Community service and political-moral identity in adolescents. *Journal of Research on Adolescence*, *6*(3), 271–284; Yates, M., & Youniss, J. (1998). Community service and political identity development in adolescence. *Journal of Social Issues*, *54*(3), 495–512; Youniss, J., & Yates, M. (1999). Youth service and moral-civic identity: A case for everyday morality. *Educational Psychology Review*, *11*(4), 361–376.

14. Catalano et al. (2002); Flanagan. (2004); Larson. (1993). Youth organizations, hobbies, and sports as developmental contexts. In R. K. Silbereisen & E. Todt (Eds.), *Adolescence in context: The interplay of family, school, peers, and work in adjustment* (pp. 46–65). New York: Springer-Verlag.

15. Coffey, A., & Atkinson, P. (1996). *Making sense of qualitative data*. Thousand Oaks, CA: Sage; Denzin, N. K., & Lincoln, Y. S. (2003). Introduction: The discipline and practice of qualitative research. In N. K. Denzin & Y. S. Lincoln (Eds.), *The landscape of qualitative research: Theories and issues* (pp. 1–45). Thousand Oaks, CA: Sage.

16. The names of all organizations and individuals, with the exception of myself, have been changed to protect their anonymity.

17. Marshall, C., & Rossman, G. B. (1999). *Designing qualitative research*. Thousand Oaks, CA: Sage.

18. Erickson, F. (1986). Qualitative methods in research on teaching. In M. Wittrock (Ed.), *Handbook of research on teaching* (3rd ed., pp. 119–161). New York: Macmillan; Huberman, L. (1994). *Qualitative data analysis: An expanded sourcebook* (2nd ed.). Thousand Oaks, CA: Sage.

19. A sample set of youths' self-descriptions was given to a second coder for a reliability check. We coded for both connected and individuated self. Kappas were .88 to .89.

20. Strauss, A., & Corbin, J. (1994). Grounded theory methodology: An overview. In N. K. Denzin & Y. S. Lincoln (Eds.), *Handbook of qualitative research* (pp. 273–285). Thousand Oaks, CA: Sage.

21. All words were coded within the context of the individual participant's response. Some words may be coded differently for different youth. For example, *athletic* used in the context of having talent in sports would be coded as individual. *Athletic* discussed with regard to being a team player would be coded as connected.

22. Hart et al. (1998).

23. Lawrence-Lightfoot, S. (2000). *Respect*. Cambridge, MA: Perseus Books.

24. DeFrancisco, V. L., & Chatham-Carpenter, A. (2000). Self in community: African American women's views of self-esteem. *Howard Journal of Communications, 11*, 73–92.

25. Strausberg, C. (2003). Atty Meyers to churches: Form armies of black males to teach youths "code of honor." *Chicago Defender*, 3; Worrill, C. W. (2001). Taking a deeper look at ourselves. *Michigan Citizen, 23*(46), A7.

26. Stevens, J. W. (1997). African American female adolescent identity development: A three-dimensional perspective. *Child Welfare, 76*(1), 145–173; Dimitriadis, G. (2001). Border identities, transformed lives, and danger zones: The mediation of validated selves, friendship networks, and successful paths in community-based organizations. *Discourse: Studies in the Cultural Politics of Education, 22*(3), 361–374.

27. Hemmings, A. (2002). Youth culture of hostility: Discourses of money, respect, and difference. *Qualitative Studies in Education, 15*(3), 291–307.

28. Bourgois, P. I. (1995). *In search of respect: Selling crack in El Barrio*. Cambridge: Cambridge University Press; Bowman, P. J. (1995). Family structure and the marginalization of black men: Commentary. In M. B. Tucker & C.

Mitchell-Keman (Eds.), *The decline in marriage among African Americans: Causes, consequences, and policy implications* (pp. 309–321). New York: Russell Sage Foundation.

29. Hemmings, A. (2002). Youth culture of hostility: Discourses of money, respect, and difference. *Qualitative Studies in Education, 15*(3), 291–307; Bourgois. (1995); Bowman. (1995); Burton, L. M., Allison, K. W., & Obeidallah, D. (1995). Social context and adolescence: Perspectives on development among inner-city African-American teens. In L. J. Crockett & A. C. Crouter (Eds.), *Pathways through adolescence: Individual development in relation to social contexts* (pp. 119–138). Mahwah, NJ: Erlbaum; Seaton, G. (2004, Mar.). *Coping across context: The functionality of Black hypermasculinity.* Paper presented at the Society for Research on Adolescence, Baltimore, MD.

30. Lawrence-Lightfoot. (2000).

31. DeFrancisco & Chatham-Carpenter. (2000).

32. Damon, W. (1998). Political development for a democratic future: A commentary. *Journal of Social Issues, 54*(3), 621–628.

33. Lawrence-Lightfoot. (2000); Britt, D. (1999); Aspy, D. N., Roebuck, F. N., & Black, B. (1972). The relationship of teacher-offered conditions of respect to behaviors described by Flanders' interaction analysis. *Journal of Negro Education, 41*(4), 370–376.

34. Aspy et al. (1972).

35. Hart et al. (1998).

36. Resistance to one-sided respect must be understood within the cultural-historical framework of African Americans and other minorities in America. For discussion, see Deutsch, N. L. (2005). There are birds in the projects: The construction of self in an urban youth organization. *Dissertation Abstracts International,* Section B: *The Physical Sciences and Engineering, 65*(12), 6706.

37. McAdams, D. P., & Bowman, P. J. (2001). Narrating life's turning points: Redemption and contamination. In D. P. McAdams, R. Josselson, & A. Lieblich (Eds.), *Turns in the road: Studies of lives in transition* (pp. 3–34). Washington, DC: American Psychological Association; McAdams, D. P., Diamond, A., de St. Aubin, E., & Mansfield, E. (1997). Stories of commitment: The psychosocial construction of generative lives. *Journal of Personality and Social Psychology, 72*(3), 678–694.

38. Hart et al. (1998); Reimer. (2003); Nasir & Kirshner. (2003); Damon, W., Menon, J., & Bronk, K. C. (2003). The development of purpose during adolescence. *Applied Developmental Science, 7*(3), 119–128.

39. Colby & Damon. (1995).

40. Flanagan. (2004).

41. Walker, L. J. (2004). What does moral functioning entail? In T. A. Thorkildsen & H. J. Walberg (Eds.), *Nurturing morality issues in children's and families' lives* (pp. 3–17). New York: Kluwer Academic/Plenum.

NANCY L. DEUTSCH *is an assistant professor of educational leadership, foundations, and policy at the University of Virginia's Curry School of Education.*

If learning is a social process, then youngsters need more than academic instruction. The authors describe a method for helping youth to develop caring and concern for others, establish positive relationships, and make responsible decisions.

7

Promoting children's ethical development through social and emotional learning

Elizabeth Devaney, Mary Utne O'Brien,
Mary Tavegia, Hank Resnik

ALTHOUGH FEW EDUCATORS, youth development practitioners, and student support services personnel question the importance of helping children to develop the skills necessary to be successful in the workplace, make ethical decisions, and be engaged and contributing citizens, these skills are rarely taught explicitly and effectively. The pressures of accountability for student performance, accelerated by the requirements of the No Child Left Behind Act of 2002, lead educators to focus solely on improving test scores in the core areas of reading and mathematics. Today's out-of-school-time programming is also overwhelmingly under pressure to maintain an academic focus. This focus on testing means that too often, academic subjects are divorced from the social context in which they are taught. Educators feel they must choose between teaching content or teaching character; between engaging students in the

NEW DIRECTIONS FOR YOUTH DEVELOPMENT, NO. 108, WINTER 2005 © WILEY PERIODICALS, INC.

study of great literature or nurturing great values; between preparing for high-stakes tests or preparing for the high-stakes tasks of learning to cooperate with peers, avoiding risk-taking behaviors, and engaging in positive civic activities.

In 2003, the Search Institute highlighted why we can no longer afford to choose academics over social, emotional, and ethical development.[1] Its surveys of youth indicate that:

- 29 percent feel that they think through the consequences of their choices and plan ahead—but 71 percent do not.
- 35 percent say that they respect the values and beliefs of people from different races and cultures—but 65 percent do not.
- 24 percent report feeling that their teachers really care about them—but 76 percent do not.

Many educators and other youth development practitioners recognize that social, emotional, and ethical skills development cannot be ignored in the name of better academic preparation. They know learning is a social process: children do not learn alone but rather in collaboration with teachers and other adults, in the company of their peers, and with the support of their families. Emotions can facilitate or hamper their learning and, ultimately, their success in school and life. But while many who work with youth understand this, they have had little support to help them combine social, emotional, and academic learning.

All of this is changing. Twenty years of research show that efforts to promote children's social and emotional competence have had substantial impacts on educational motivation, behavior, risk taking, and attachment to school. Recent research has demonstrated that in the process, social and emotional learning (SEL) programming also improves academic performance.

What is SEL?

Social and emotional learning, a concept formally introduced by the Collaborative for Academic, Social, and Emotional Learning

(CASEL) in the book *Promoting Social and Emotional Learning: Guidelines for Educators,* provides educators, both in and out of schools, with a way to address the needs of all students by teaching critical skills for success in school and life, while still focusing on their primary academic mission.[2]

SEL is the process of acquiring the skills to recognize and manage emotions, develop caring and concern for others, establish positive relationships, make responsible decisions, and handle challenging situations effectively. Research has shown that SEL has an impact on every aspect of children's development: their health, ethical development, citizenship, academic learning, and motivation to achieve.[3] Figure 7.1 highlights five key areas of social and emotional competency that CASEL has identified as essential for children's social, emotional, and ethical functioning:

In other words, if our schools, after-school programs, and youth development agencies work together to help young people to be self-aware, manage their emotions, be aware of others, have good

Figure 7.1. Five SEL competency areas

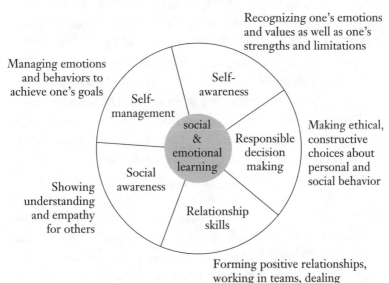

relationships skills, and solve problems effectively, we have equipped them with the skills they need to live ethically and responsibly. The good news is that these skills can be taught, and many excellent evidence-based programs that help children develop such skills are available.[4] SEL is more than a program, however. It is an approach to educating children that starts in the classroom but quickly moves beyond it to the lunchroom, the playground, the playing fields, summer programs, and the home.[5]

An illustration of successful SEL implementation

Cossitt Elementary School in LaGrange, Illinois, began implementing SEL programming more than nine years ago. With 580 students in grades pre-K through 6, Cossitt is a school where children feel safe, comfortable, and happy and where, after many years of careful and thoughtful programming, SEL has reached into every corner of the school community.

Cossitt's SEL work stems from a carefully planned implementation effort. A team of parents, teachers, and administrators worked together to conduct a needs assessment and select an evidence-based SEL program. By unanimous decision, the team chose the nationally recognized and well-researched Child Development Project (CDP; later revised and renamed Caring School Community CSC).[6] The program was a starting point for what would become a much bigger and more integrated approach to SEL in the school.

Central to the adoption and success of CDP was the school team's support of the program's central values and core beliefs. Those values and beliefs, which Cossitt has developed into its own mission, continue to be a strong guide for the educational process at Cossitt today:

Children learn through relationships. Just as anyone who feels part of a community will uphold the values of that community and promote the well-being of its members, so children who feel they belong to a caring community of learners will value learning and each other as individuals.

Intellectual, ethical, and social learning are not independent. Each affects the others.

Children from all social, economic, and cultural backgrounds are learners—and a caring community of learners includes all children.

Children want to learn, and will learn when presented with a challenging, engaging curriculum.

Learning must relate to children's lives. It should connect to the issues that matter to them and that confront them—such as how to be a good friend, how to play fair, how to be both "nice" and honest, and what it means to do a good job.

When children work together, emphasizing collaboration more than competition, they learn more, feel better about themselves and their classmates, like school, and enjoy learning.

The first year: A critical turning point

The teachers at Cossitt entered the first year of CDP implementation with high expectations for the program and great enthusiasm. As described in a report evaluating their efforts, "The August training of the entire teaching and support staff generated a deep well of trust in one another and shared understanding and unity about the kind of environment staff wanted for themselves as teaching professionals and for their students. Many described it as 'a gift' just to be invited to think about and articulate broader visions about the school environment and the long-term purpose of their classroom activities."[7]

Despite their enthusiasm, after several months the adults at Cossitt were disappointed that the new program was not creating the kinds of changes in the school they had envisioned. Looking back on this early phase from the vantage point of many years, staff members now refer to this experience with self-mocking humor. "We kept waiting for kids' behavior to magically change, and it didn't in dramatic ways," says one. "In fact, for many kids it was a struggle and a time for testing their new role in the school."

According to principal Mary Tavegia:

The fall of 1997 was a major turning point for the staff. People were saying, "Why aren't these kids changing?" We were doing a great deal of reflecting on the process at our staff meetings, and finally we had a group "aha!" We realized we expected the children to change—but not ourselves as educators. We'd been thinking the program would work if we "'fixed" the children, but we realized we were the ones who had to change—and then the children's behavior would change, too. That was a major awareness for us.

The "group 'aha!'" was a critical step in moving the project forward. As one teacher observed, although they might have encouraged students to assist in developing classroom rules prior to CDP, they would have viewed it as a way of exercising control over the children. Under the new approach, they came to think of it as a way of encouraging children to take responsibility for their own behavior and learning. This shift was both subtle and profound. As one teacher recalls:

At first I found giving up some control and allowing students more autonomy personally challenging, but I've learned to take these risks. When we started the program I was a fairly new teacher. I was still trying to get a handle on classroom management, but I've been so pleased with the results. Adding SEL has made a huge difference in my teaching and is a big part of who I am as a teacher today.

SEL today

Today, SEL is seamlessly integrated into everything that happens at Cossitt. Take a stroll through the halls, peek into the classrooms, or step onto the playground, and you are likely to see any one of the following. All are based on actual recent observations at Cossitt:

Class meetings. Second graders and their teacher gather together on the carpeted floor of a classroom for "morning meeting." The student leader for the day asks everyone to use a "butterfly greeting," welcoming the classmates to their left and right. The students practice skills they have learned as part of the school's SEL programming, including using eye contact, body language, and an appropriate tone of voice. The student leader follows this with sharing time. She starts by telling what she did over the weekend. Other students ask follow-up questions about her weekend to show they have been using active listening skills. The meeting ends with a "telegraph" activity: students send a message around the circle using hand squeezes. After finishing the activity, they talk briefly about how messages can get distorted. During the meeting, students "check themselves" to correct any inappropriate behavior, a primary means of classroom management. On several occasions, the teacher asks, "Could you check yourself . . ." followed by various specifics, such as, "to make sure you're sitting with your legs crossed like we agreed?" Throughout, the students are practicing a variety of skills and behaviors—listening, communicating effectively, showing respect for others—that they have learned through SEL lessons. Morning meetings are a way of life at Cossitt and a key to creating a caring community.

Conflict resolution. On the playground during recess, some fourth graders get into a conflict. One of them, a troubled child who lives with his family in a domestic violence shelter affiliated with the school, has been calling the others names and disrupting their game. Another student in the group approaches the boy and talks to him calmly. "You don't have to be like that here," he says. "This is a caring place. We'll take care of you here."

Graphic evidence of how SEL governs relationships within this community of learners. Every classroom features its own student-generated norms for discipline and behavior, "Ways We Want Our Class to Be," and rules for working with a partner in cooperative projects ("don't interrupt," "use nice words," "don't fool around," "do your share," "don't moan and groan if you're not with your best friend"). Other posters and student art work highlight values such as friendship, responsibility, respect, and kindness. Students' messages to each other say, "I believe in you." "I'm glad you're you." "I trust you." "You're important." "You're listened to." "You're cared for." and "Believe in yourself." There are photographs of the students with statements they have written about things they like to do—a way of promoting understanding and respect for others. In the hallways is evidence of "buddy" activities between older and younger students, including graphs and charts comparing height, hair color, and other physical features of the buddy pairs that promote awareness of and respect for others.

Integrated SEL programming. SEL and academic learning are integrated in a variety of ways. For every lesson, teachers develop academic content objectives and SEL objectives. For example, literature and social studies lessons may focus on themes in stories or historical events that are related to SEL issues such as decision making, accepting responsibility for one's behavior, and showing caring and concern for others. Discussion of these themes often spills over into student writing and reflection. In math and science, teachers create opportunities for students to work collaboratively and learn how to communicate and take responsibility. SEL is also integrated into activities outside the classroom. On a regular basis, children are given "home-side" activities that ask them to engage a family member in an interactive assignment. The school runs a support group for students who have been affected by death or divorce. Art, music, and physical education class all incorporate SEL themes such as cooperation, empathy, and relationship skills.

Calm and orderly students. Two teachers are talking in the hallway. One is telling the other about a school trip the day before to the Art Institute in downtown Chicago. She reports proudly that she was stopped four times by people commenting on how impressed they were with the students; they had never seen such an engaged group of children interacting so well together. In general, teachers at Cossitt feel they have more time to dedicate to classroom instruction since SEL has taken hold at the school. Referrals to the office are virtually nonexistent, and petty classroom disruptions are rare. Students often work out conflict among themselves, freeing the teachers to focus on the important tasks of learning.

Looking toward the future

For years, individual teachers, after-school program directors, coaches, and parent volunteers have endeavored to address children's social, emotional, and ethical development, without the kind of support and infrastructure afforded those in the Cossitt Elementary School community. Some have even faced active opposition from those who see such programming as too "soft" or a waste of time. In fact, the attention and priority Cossitt has placed on

SEL is the main reason for its success in creating a school community where children behave in caring and mutually supportive ways, so that students are safe to learn to the peak of their ability.

The Cossitt experience does not have to be unique. More and more people are beginning to recognize the importance of social and emotional development. At the state level, Illinois passed the Children's Mental Health Act in 2003 requiring the state board of education to develop SEL learning standards and all school districts to incorporate them into their educational plans. On a smaller scale, the strategies Cossitt uses can be applied in other school settings as well as nonschool environments. For example, the concept of morning meeting can be translated into a ten-minute session at the beginning of sports practice, play rehearsal, or summer camp. Norms for behavior can be developed by any gathering of children and adults to create an atmosphere of respect and shared responsibility. Cooperative, team-building games and activities can take the place of competition. Even competition can be recast as competing to reach one's highest potential (in which case a tough competitor is valued and respected) rather than to humiliate or destroy an opponent. Mentoring programs, sports camps, art and music programs, and after-school tutoring all offer opportunities to incorporate SEL, often at little or no additional cost—and with only the extra effort required to be purposeful and deliberate about addressing social and emotional development for ethical and effective behavior. Cossitt offers an illustration of the impact SEL can have on both the adults and the children in a learning community. Although the effects of SEL will not manifest themselves overnight, it is time for more focused support of efforts to equip children with not only the academic skills they need to achieve success but also the social and emotional competence to wield that knowledge responsibly, effectively, and ethically.

Notes

1. Benson, P. L., Scales, P. C., & Roehlkepartain, E. C. (1999). *A fragile foundation: The state of developmental assets among American youth.* Minneapolis, MN: Search Institute.

2. Elias, M., Zins, J., Weissberg, R., Frey, K., Greenberg, M., Haynes, N., Kessler, R., Schwab-Stone, M. E., & Shriver, T. P. (1997). *Promoting social and emotional learning: Guidelines for educators.* Alexandria, VA: ASCD.

3. Zins, J., Weissberg, R., Wang, M., & Walberg, H. (Eds.). (2004). *Building academic success on social and emotional learning: What the research says.* New York: Teachers College Press.

4. Collaborative for Academic, Social, and Emotional Learning. (2003). *Safe and sound: An educational leader's guide to evidence-based social and emotional learning (SEL) programs.* Chicago: Author.

5. Devaney, E., O'Brien, M. U., Resnik, R., Keister, S., & Weissberg, R. (2005). *Steps to safe and sound schools: An implementation guide and tool kit for sustainable, school-wide social and emotional learning.* Chicago: Collaborative for Academic, Social, and Emotional Learning.

6. Battistich, V., Schaps, E., Watson, M., & Solomon, D. (1996). Prevention effects of the Child Development Project: Early findings from an ongoing multisite demonstration trial. *Journal of Early Adolescence, 11,* 12–35.

7. O'Brien, M. U., & Murray, J. R. (2000, Spring). *School environments, student life, and the Child Development Project in School District 102: 1996–1999.* Evaluation report submitted to the Lagrange, Illinois District.

ELIZABETH DEVANEY *is a project director at the Collaborative for Academic, Social, and Emotional Learning (CASEL) at the University of Illinois at Chicago.*

MARY UTNE O'BRIEN *is the executive director of CASEL and a research professor of education and psychology at the University of Illinois at Chicago.*

MARY TAVEGIA *is the principal of Cossitt Elementary School, District 102, LaGrange, Illinois.*

HANK RESNIK *is an independent education consultant.*

*What strategies can help transform the attitudes
and behaviors of youth who have low self-esteem,
few resources, and little interest in learning?*

8

Giving youth the social and emotional skills to succeed

Ginny Deerin

DEREK JOHNSON (not his real name) arrived at the WINGS for Kids after-school program as a third grader who disrupted class, neglected homework, and defied his teachers. He clowned, cursed, tripped other students, and flagrantly disobeyed the rules. Once he climbed onto the roof at school and threw rocks from above. Fistfights were routine. And his aggression was not confined to classmates. One day he took a swing at a WINGS leader, knocking her against a row of lockers and breaking the watch she was wearing. "He was a little thug," says Tamara Field, the counselor whom Derek shoved in a rage.

Yet this troubled eight-year-old boy was able to shed his self-destructive behavior and remake himself into a responsible young man with a promising future. His schoolwork advanced so much that by sixth grade, he was singled out as the most improved student in the class. He got help for reading difficulties that had gone undetected at school or at home. He began to manage his anger, value his strengths and recognize his weaknesses, experience empathy, and communicate constructively with friends and family. He

NEW DIRECTIONS FOR YOUTH DEVELOPMENT, NO. 108, WINTER 2005 © WILEY PERIODICALS, INC.

learned how to cope with the difficulties that so many disadvantaged youth must face.

By acquiring these social and emotional skills in small lessons woven throughout his afterschool activities, Derek improved his academic performance and his ability to distinguish right from wrong. His story demonstrates the power of social and emotional learning to shape the ethical as well as the personal and academic lives of children.

Missing a piece of their education

WINGS provides a framework of strategies, practices, and materials for social and emotional learning (SEL) to take place within afterschool programs. Founded in Charleston, South Carolina, in 1996 as a nonprofit organization and developed in partnerships that field-tested and strengthened these educational interventions in summer camps and elementary schools serving predominantly poor, African American youth as well as an after-school program for adolescents housed in an abandoned firehouse, WINGS grew out of my personal conviction that children were missing an important piece in their education.

I had experienced considerable success as a marketing and fundraising executive, helping businesses flourish and politicians get elected to statewide office. Yet I found myself struggling in middle age with personal challenges that tested my emotional resources. My six-year-old daughter's father—my ex-husband— was dying of cancer. I struggled to help her cope. In a search for assistance, I spent time with psychologists, read all the research I could find, studied, and began acquiring new skills. Out of my own struggle grew my resolve to help children develop the capabilities to navigate life's social and emotional difficulties.

In these days of tremendous political pressure for results measured by standardized tests, time constraints can make SEL a difficult undertaking for many classroom teachers. It seemed to me that after-school programs would be effective learning environments for supplying the missing piece in children's education.

Developing SEL in small lessons

The WINGS elementary school program begins when the school day ends. Ours is not a drop-in program; the students attend fifteen hours each week—three hours a day. We serve 120 children who attend Memminger Elementary School in the heart of Charleston's historic district. These students averaged 42.5 percent below basic in English language arts and 36.1 percent below basic in math, with 96 percent qualifying for free or reduced lunch in 2004. The time is divided: five hours devoted to homework and academics, five hours of choice time, three hours of playground and free time, one hour of community service, and one hour of what we call WildWINGS— a special activity at week's end. Students make new choices every nine weeks, selecting activities that include dance, computer, reading and writing clubs, art, African drumming, etiquette, chess, gardening, board games, basketball, and rap club.

All of these activities are infused with intentional and carefully conceived social and emotional lessons. For example, the planning of a nine-week dance program maps out for each lesson specific SEL objectives to be taught along with movement skills. The staff focuses on teaching young people how to give positive feedback to other dancers as they try new steps or strengthening the listening skills of the dancers so that choreography instructions are heard and respected. It is through these small lessons taught during the course of ordinary activity that children acquire and practice their new skills with the support of staff members who receive constant training and reinforcement in their own social and emotional skills.

Through trial and error, the program staff of WINGS have developed five learning modules for successful SEL strategies, practices, and materials:

- Community Unity helps build a caring community through specific social and emotional skills.
- Staff Shapers enhance the teaching and SEL-specific skills of WINGS program leaders.
- SELementary shows how to teach SEL basics in engaging ways.
- Bring It In provides activities and tools to integrate SEL into an after-school program every day.
- You Rule gives staff techniques and tools to help manage behavior.

This is an approach that can add value to existing after-school activities and programs. For example, a typical youth leader teaches children how to hit a baseball, while a youth leader uses WINGS to also teach how to handle their feelings if they swing and miss the ball. A typical tutor drills students in preparation for a math test; with WINGS methods, that tutor would also help them deal with pretest jitters.

_____

Looking at one boy's struggle

The information and comments at the beginning of this chapter and those that follow about Derek, his family, and how WINGS helped him were gathered in interviews conducted by a writer who was brought in by one of our funders.[1] The writer had the permission of Derek and his mother to tell their story. (All names have been changed for this chapter.) While we work closely with parents and often hear details of their circumstances, we typically do not collect personal information about WINGS children in such detail.

Derek's mother, Alice, was only a freshman in high school when he was born. Herself the child of a teenage mother, Alice struggled to stay in school, care for her baby, and work at McDonald's to help pay the bills. When her second boy was born in her senior year, she reluctantly dropped out.

"I loved learning. It was so hard to leave," she says. Her anger, like her burdens, grew. While Alice worked long hours managing a sandwich shop at the hospital, Derek sometimes had to feed and dress himself and his younger brother and travel across town by bus to reach school. He was close to his father, who was trying, with limited success, to leave behind a past that included jail time for drug possession. When the boy was seven, Derek's father vanished after a beating that police believe was administered as punishment for an old drug dispute. His body has never been found. There were numerous moves because rent money was hard to come by, and the death of a beloved grandmother contributed to the family's instability.

Derek's difficulties in school began to grow. "He fought all the time. He had aggressiveness," his mother says. "It seemed like no one could say anything to him. He was using profane language. He was late to school all the time."

Full of rage, Derek lashed out with his fists. "I used to get in fights if kids would run down my family. They would make fun of how you read or do your work," he recalls.

Derek got off to a bad start when he arrived at WINGS at the age of eight. Sent to a chair to cool off on the first day after a dispute, he stood drop-kicking it against the wall for fun instead of sitting in it. More than once he had to be physically restrained to keep from hurting someone. For a time, he was ejected from the WINGS program for refusing to abide by the rules that keep children safe.

The WINGS leaders never gave up on Derek, and they made it clear to him what he had to do to return. He was belligerent in response. But they noticed that the cocky boy so disdainful of their authority was often turning up on the periphery of WINGS activities. He would stand at a distance, watching wistfully while students played games on the playground. And after several months, he earned his way back into the program with a commitment to change.

Controlling anger on the basketball court

Learning to manage his emotions made a huge difference in Derek's behavior. An avid ball player, we found that many of his best learnings occurred on the basketball court. He benefited especially from one of the most effective practices we teach our staff: the art of dialoguing to express empathy without passing judgment.

An example is when Derek exploded in a rage in the middle of a game over what he considered an unfair call. He yelled disrespectfully at the coach. A WINGS leader intervened and asked Derek to go for a walk to talk privately. Here is how their conversation went:

LEADER: Hey, Derek, what's up with this behavior?

DEREK: Nothing.

LEADER: Hmmm. (Long, reflective pause.)

DEREK: That call was stupid. The coach is stupid. That call was wrong!

LEADER: So you thought he made a bad call.

DEREK: Yeah, he doesn't know what he's doing. He sucks. He can't play basketball. I don't know why WINGS has him do basketball. He sucks.

LEADER: You don't think he's the guy to be in charge of basketball.

DEREK: Yeah, he sucks.

LEADER: So you really don't think he's doing a good job.

DEREK: No.

LEADER: Is there more you want to say about this?

DEREK: Nah. He just sucks.

LEADER: Well, Derek, I'll bet you are feeling pretty angry. Have I got that right?

DEREK: Yeah.

Derek feels that he is heard and understood, which diffuses his anger. Just because the WINGS leader listened carefully to Derek does not mean he endorses his disrespectful behavior. In this case, since it was near the end of the day, he told Derek that the next day they would get together to do some problem solving to discuss other actions he could have taken in the same situation to express his anger in a more constructive way.

There were many more opportunities during basketball games to build Derek's confidence and his emotional capabilities. As he took small steps toward breaking his negative habits, WINGS leaders frequently made note of the times he refrained from outbursts or conflicts and praised his growing self-control.

Building confidence and self-esteem

Derek always loved Fridays because it was time for WildWINGS, something new and different each week centered on a theme and loaded with SEL. One week it was "You Bug Me!—activities that included games, discussion, and role playing.

The learning objectives are to teach awareness of the relationship between thoughts, feelings, and actions and how that dynamic assists in managing impulses; demonstrate alternative emotional responses; predict consequences and choose their best solutions; and practice expressing feelings and ideas assertively without aggression. We want children to internalize these lessons: "I can work out my problems with people." "When someone is bugging me, I can be patient." I won't get upset over little things." We let them act out all kinds of hypothetical situations by taking turns drawing what we call "bugger situations" from a container. What if they are in class and the "bugger" taunts, "Your mama is stupid." What is the best response?

WINGS leaders point out some do's and don'ts, with help from the participants. Don't push or hit out of anger when someone insults your mother. Asked for some other ways to handle the "bugger," one child offers this response: "Look, if you've got a problem with my mama, that's your problem and not mine. I think my mama is real smart. If you don't—tell her yourself!"

At the same time that young people like Derek are receiving very specific instructions in how to manage anger in real-life situations, they are constantly receiving positive feedback for achievements and improvements. WINGS staff dole out raffle tickets when they catch children making progress as they develop these skills, and at week's end the winner whose ticket is chosen wins the video version of *A Bug's Life* or some other prize that is a fun reminder of their progress.

One staff activity focuses on giving and receiving compliments, emphasizing that it is extremely effective to express admiration for traits, characteristics. and actions of WINGS students and their leaders.

Derek's growing capabilities to be attuned to his own needs enabled him to admit what none of his teachers or family members had detected: that he was struggling with reading deficiencies. That allowed him to get remedial help. As his reading gradually improved, he began to overcome the sense of inadequacy that prompted the constant fights and the need to swagger.

"He's like a totally different kid," says Tamara Field, the WINGS leader whom Derek once intimidated. Now she beams with pride over his accomplishments: "He realizes everybody has strengths and weaknesses. He's got a lot to work on, but he's not trying to impress anybody anymore. He's not afraid he will look dumb when he asks questions. He helps the other kids. He helps me. Now he sees what strength really is."

"I was so proud of him that he could change his attitude. It was amazing!" says another WINGS leader, Fred Jones. "He was definitely headed for big trouble. The temptations of the street were everywhere around him, and many of his family members went the wrong way. But he's grown into a bright young man who's got such a mature spirit."

The other students consider Derek a leader who is both cool and kind. He works hard on his homework, peacefully resolves his disputes on the basketball court, and treats adults with respect. A freshman now attending a magnet high school, his eyes shine with excitement when he talks of attending college and maybe pursuing a career building houses or caring for animals someday.

Helping youth feel safe, valued, confident

At WINGS we see over and over that many behavioral problems presented by children like Derek stem from a lack of success in the classroom that causes them to question their self worth.

Early evaluations of this approach by University of South Carolina researchers over the past seven years have shown statistically significant outcomes, with high satisfaction levels among participants that result in after-school attendance rates above 95 percent, improved report card grades, increased parental involvement, and a highly motivated staff with a low turnover rate that has prompted other youth programs like Boys and Girls Clubs to seek our training assistance.[2]

Research now under way by the Health, Emotion, and Behavior Laboratory at Yale University will analyze the data gathered at WINGS since its inception. Because WINGS strategies, practices, and materials can be easily replicated at relatively low cost, these educational interventions could potentially add value to a wide variety of afterschool programs. In the 2005–2006 school year, we will refine these methodologies and test their accessibility through the integration of WINGS practices in five new developmental partnerships with existing after-school programs—two programs in Washington, D.C., and two additional programs in Charleston— all of them serving mostly low-income students—as well as a fifth school in Charleston serving middle-—to upper-income students.

It is unrealistic to expect these youth to become responsible citizens who make ethical choices if they have not learned to manage their emotions and cultivate self-awareness. With an appreciation of their personal strengths that comes from social and emotional learning, they can develop the motivation to succeed in school and have positive social engagement with their peers and their communities.

In order to lead joyful, responsible, fulfilling lives, all children deserve a strong social and emotional education. But for students like Derek who arrive at overburdened inner-city schools with multiple disadvantages and scant resources, the development of these capabilities is not just important. It is crucial.

Notes

1. Schwed, P. (2002). *Connecting strengths, creating change. 2002 WINGS Annual Report.* Arthur M. Blank Family Foundation, Atlanta, GA.

2. Linney, J., & Spelman, E. (2001–2004). *Wings for kids program evaluation.* Unpublished manuscript, University of South Carolina.

GINNY DEERIN *is founder and CEO of Wings for Kids, Inc.*

A university extension and its partners launched a program to provide training, promotional efforts, and recognition to make good sportsmanship the norm rather than the exception in connection with competition in sports and other arenas.

9

Developing a game plan for good sportsmanship

Kathleen Lodl

INVOLVEMENT IN COMPETITIVE events such as athletics, speech, drama, music, and 4-H is a cornerstone in most communities in the United States. We are a nation that thrives on participation in competition. While it is often thought that such participation builds good character, it does not automatically happen. Just as a coach has a plan for each game and for the season, we need to develop a plan for learning good character and sportsmanship through all extracurricular activities. By developing such a plan, we can be better assured that competition can be an experience that more fully contributes to positive youth development. This chapter focuses on one example of such a program, "Great Fans. Great Sports."

Research indicates that competition can be an important context whereby youth gain positive outcomes such as intrinsic motivation and engagement in the environment.[1] However, other studies indicate that sports activities may also relate to negative outcomes such as aggression[2] and cheating.[3] One of the challenges for educators and youth development professionals is to help create competitive

NEW DIRECTIONS FOR YOUTH DEVELOPMENT, NO. 108, WINTER 2005 © WILEY PERIODICALS, INC.

environments where positive outcomes are strengthened and negative behaviors are lessened.

This is no easy task. The media are full of examples of fans and players out of control. In 2004, Texas Ranger pitcher Frank Francisco threw a chair into the stadium and broke a woman's nose. In 1997, NBA star Dennis Rodman was suspended for kicking a sportside photographer. The problem of unsportsmanlike conduct has gotten so severe that in November 2004, *ABC Nightline* dedicated a program to aggression at sporting events.[4] Examples of poor sportsmanship go beyond the players and beyond athletics. In summer 2005, a youth league in New Bedford, Massachusetts, was stopped because of fighting parents. *Parade* magazine has run a story on youth sports, emphasizing parents' misplaced priorities. The Bravo Network introduced *Sports Kids Moms and Dads*, a reality show that focuses on five families, each striving to make their child into a star, no matter what the cost. All of these examples run contrary to encouraging competitive participation for the development of such traits as teamwork, responsibility, and self-control—and certainly, take away the fun.

Noted experts in character development surmise that to be effective, ethical development must be a systemic, communitywide effort that encompasses how we teach in schools, conduct extracurricular activities, operate our businesses, run community organizations, and as individuals function on a day-to-day basis.[5] An approach to building ethical understanding and strong character is outlined by Michael Josephson, founder of the Josephson Institute of Ethics and the Character Counts! program. Josephson surmises that through extracurricular activities, young people can be taught the six pillars of character: trustworthiness, respect, responsibility, fairness, caring, and citizenship.[6]

"Great Fans. Great Sports." is a program designed to develop these character traits in all areas of competition. The "Great Sports" portion of the title refers not just to sports but to sportsmanship in the broadest sense. From the basketball court to the music auditorium to the rodeo arena to the debate room, the project partners—the University of Nebraska–Lincoln Extension, the

University of Nebraska Alumni Association, and the Nebraska School Activities Association—had the vision for creating a positive competitive environment for participants, parents, fans, coaches, and the community while promoting ethical development among young people. "Great Fans. Great Sports." uses the six pillars of Character Counts! to help instill good sportsmanship as the norm, not the exception.

How it works

Communities interested in "Great Fans. Great Sports." choose from a variety of online tools (www.greatfansgreatsports.com) to develop a local plan as to how they can most effectively implement strategies that will foster character development throughout their community. These local plans involve competitive events that take place in schools, through service organizations (for example, American Legion Baseball, National High School Rodeo Association), and through youth-serving organizations (for example, Boy Scouts, YMCA, 4-H). This local-level design allows communities to develop a plan that fits the competitive interests of their community. For example, one community may focus primarily on basketball, while another designs its program around the rodeo season or the local Miss Teen pageant.

"Great Fans. Great Sports." is designed to run on a budget of any size. Some communities hire people to lead the training and oversee the program, while others rely on community volunteers. Some have a large budget for developing promotional materials and giving away "freebies" to promote the program; others get local businesses to sponsor ads or support giveaways. One community has budgeted dollars into booster club dues to cover the cost of "Great Fans. Great Sports" T-shirts for students. Another has written to a local community foundation for support.

Communities participating in "Great Fans. Great Sports." begin the competitive season (whether it be sports, drama, or 4-H) with a meeting of coaches, participants, and parents. During this initial meeting, expectations for participation are developed—for example, practice and attendance expectations, equipment requirements, rules for participation, and expectations for behavior at competitive events. In the most successful settings, codes of sportsmanship are developed and signed by participants, parents, and coaches. This creates a sense of ownership for the outcomes of the season and a clear vision of operating principles.

Educational programs for coaches, parents, and youth held throughout the competitive cycle focus on what good sportsmanship looks like in that particular competitive event and how good character can be promoted. Hands-on activities, case studies, and ideas for instilling good sportsmanship are covered.

In addition to the training, communities develop a promotional plan for encouraging good sportsmanship. For example, public service announcements focusing on good sportsmanship are made prior to and during the season for competitive events. These announcements focus on the commitment of that community to promote good sportsmanship and positive character development through competition. Codes of conduct and sportsmanship creeds are included in event programs and posted where the competition takes place.

Special "Acts of Kindness" are conducted for the opposing teams or competitors. For example, during the basketball season in one community, participants from both teams get together for shared meals before the games. In another, water or snacks are given to the opposition. Visual reminders are evident throughout competitive events. Popcorn bags, drink cups, and other concessions carry "Great Fans. Great Sports." logos. The intent is to permeate the competitive environment with the message that respect, responsibility, fairness, and caring are important—no matter what the outcome of the competition.

While most communities begin by addressing sportsmanship at the broadest level, delving into the program allows discussion of topics that might otherwise be taboo: using illegal drugs to make show animals appear calmer during competition, fans showing the same kind of support for athletic and nonathletic events, officials favoring the team that will take the most fans to the playoff game, team rivalries that have become so caustic that danger for competitors and fans is imminent. Eventually there may be opportunities to address issues of higher-order ethical conflict and allow more community discussion related to these issues. "Great Fans. Great Sports." allows the community to identify the issues most critical to it and to address hard ethical dilemmas in a nonthreatening way.

Fan-friendly communities

Communities that practice especially notable sportsmanship are eligible to apply for the Fan Friendly Community designation of "Great Fans. Great Sports." Fan Friendly Communities are those that stand out above others because of their good sportsmanship and Fan Friendly atmosphere. Criteria for being a Fan-Friendly Community include exemplifying the six pillars of character through good sportsmanship communitywide; having coaches, youth, and parents who are trained in the "Great Fans. Great Sports." program; implementing a sportsmanship code of conduct at competitive events; and documenting Acts of Kindness for opposing teams. Applications for Fan Friendly Communities are reviewed by a panel of educators, fans, and youth. Communities receiving the Fan Friendly Community designation receive special recognition and access to Fan Friendly Community logos that can be customized to suit their community. In addition, Fan Friendly Communities are recognized during a statewide celebration.

Resources

The "Great Fans. Great Sports." Web site includes curriculum and teaching outlines for youth, parents, coaches, fans, and teachers; sample sportsmanship codes; application information for Fan Friendly Community Awards; and promotional resources. In addition, the site is designed for communities to tell their story about examples of sportsmanship they have seen in communities across the state. The long-term goal is for the site to become a resource for all communities that are hoping to increase the level of sportsmanship in all competitive events.

Impact

Although it is still in its early stages, the "Great Fans. Great Sports." program appears to be making a difference in the thirty-five participating communities. At this point, results are anecdotal and have been collected through discussions with program participants and educators conducting training programs. For example, the summer youth baseball program in one community was having issues with parents' being overly critical of the players, coaches, and umpires during games. They held a series of training sessions during the summer outlining appropriate behavior and encouraging parents to put the games in perspective. As a visual cue, they handed out lollipops with labels that said: "Chew on this, not on the players." Coaches who had been considering quitting reported being treated with more respect by the parents and less negative taunting from the fans.

In another community that recently implemented training sessions for "Great Fans. Great Sports.," a 4-H volunteer leader shared that a young man had been working with his 4-H dog throughout the year in preparation for the upcoming dog show. Unfortunately, the dog was run over a month before the competition. One of the boy's fellow club members offered to let him use one of his dogs for the contest. For the month that followed, the boys, who would be competing against each other, worked together to train both dogs. The focus of the project was no longer on winning but on the relationship the boys developed and their sense of cooperation. This kind of caring helps develop the foundation for good character.

In addition to these examples, there are other results. For example, officials in communities implementing "Great Fans. Great Sports." are beginning to see decreased incidents of offensive language, fighting, and player contact. School administrators are seeing fewer referrals of student athletes. Teachers are reporting an increase in respect for other students (taking turns and patience while waiting in line) and a decrease in negative behaviors (name calling, shoving, and vulgar language).

The program is also helping to change the community culture surrounding competition. One community that had issues with parents who were "overeager" to have their children succeed developed a sportsmanship code that focused on the roles of parents as being supportive and nurturing versus demanding winning at all costs. After going through the "Great Fans. Great Sports." learning situations, several of the parents agreed that they had been overly aggressive in encouraging their children to win rather than focusing on what the activity was about. They also agreed that the expectations they had for their children might have been unrealistic.

Limitations

"Great Fans. Great Sports." has its limitations. A formal evaluation plan is in development, and only then will we know true program outcomes. We do know that without a strong community commitment to raising the sportsmanship standard, the program will not succeed. There are coaches who choose not to participate, parents who sign codes of conduct without ever planning on showing respect to the opposing teams, and organizers of competitive events who believe that closing their eyes to a situation is easier than addressing it. There are school administrators who are afraid that talking about ethical behavior will create tedious discussions at school board meetings, fans who do not believe poor sportsmanship happens in "my town," and youth who say: "I just want to win, no matter what."

Despite the downfalls, the progress is hopeful. Programs like "Great Fans. Great Sports." can change how we think about competition and how we can use it to promote positive youth development. Even if it is a small improvement, it is a step in the right direction.

Notes

1. Larson, R. W. (2000). Toward a psychology of positive youth development. *American Psychologist, 55*, 170–183.

2. Smoll, F. L., & Smith, R. E. (2002). *Children and youth in sport: A biopsychosocial perspective* (2nd ed.). Dubuque, IA: Kendall/Hunt Publishing Co.

3. Shields, D. L., Bredemeier, B. L., Gardner, D. E., & Bostrom, A. (1995). Leadership, cohesion, and team norms regarding cheating and aggression. *Sociology of Sport Journal, 12*, 324–336.

4. Sievers, L. (Executive Producer). (2004, Nov. 22). *ABC Nightline* [Television broadcast]. New York: ABC News Productions.

5. Urban, H. (2000). *Life's greatest lessons: 20 things I want my kids to know.* Saline, MI: Great Lessons Press.

6. Josephson, M. (2005). *Character counts! Implementation tool kit.* Los Angeles: Josephson Institute of Ethics.

A community collected data to determine what ado-
lescents thought about right and wrong behavior
and to identify the best venues for reaching them
outside school hours.

10

Pathways of influence in out-of-school time: A community-university partnership to develop ethics

Donna J. Peterson, James C. Roebuck,
Sherry C. Betts, Marta E. Stuart

HOW DO WE HELP youth develop ethics in this complex world? What do we know about how young people think about right and wrong? Where and when are the teachable moments? One community in the southwestern United States decided to ask youth about their ideas, values, behavior, and aspirations—in essence, put themselves in the shoes of the youth around them. They then used that information to build on strengths and address needs. This chapter describes how this community partnered with a university to use local data on what youth think about right and wrong, how they behave, and how they use out-of-school time to discover the access points or pathways of influence to promote good character and positive youth development.

NEW DIRECTIONS FOR YOUTH DEVELOPMENT, NO. 108, WINTER 2005 © WILEY PERIODICALS, INC.

Defining character and character education

Character, ethics, morals. Sometimes these words are used synonymously, while at other times they are differentiated. Howard, Berkowitz, and Schaeffer state that the field of character and moral education deals with questions of ethics and ethical behavior.[1] They argue that *character education* is now the most common term and can be used to refer to the entire field. Lickona has provided one definition of character: "Character consists of . . . values in action. Character . . . has three interrelated parts: moral knowing, moral feeling, and moral behavior. Good character consists of knowing the good, desiring the good, and doing the good—habits of the mind, habits of the heart, and habits of action. We want our children . . . to judge what is right, care deeply about what is right, and then do what they believe to be right—even in the face of pressure from without and temptation from within."[2]

While *character* is typically defined as including thoughts, feelings, and behaviors,[3] there is a great deal of literature demonstrating that people often say one thing but do another depending on the context.[4] Even as early as the 1920s, multiple experiments by Hartshorne and May that measured cheating among ten thousand children and adolescents found that adolescents could not be categorized into groups of "good character" and "bad character" based on behavior; cheating in one setting did not effectively predict cheating in another.[5] In fact, the behavior of those who said they valued honesty could not be differentiated from those who said they did not.

If we wish to incorporate parents and community members as full partners in building character among youth, then the activities and programs in which youth participate during their out-of-school time are potentially important venues. Thus, it is important to determine where youth can be reached when they are not in school and then to involve those various community partners in promoting character and positive youth development. In the study described here, a community collaboration and a subsequent community-university partnership were formed for this purpose.

Forming a collaboration for positive youth development

The setting for this project is a small southwestern city with a population of less than fifty thousand. The racial composition is overwhelmingly white—roughly 92 percent.[6] The city is served by one high school, two middle schools, and five elementary schools. It also serves as the county seat and therefore has a resident cooperative extension agent who is a faculty member of the university, concerned with youth and family issues. The extension agent serves as the liaison between the community and the university.

One of the critical reasons for forming the community-university partnership was to work together to listen to the community's young people, identify issues and assets, and find pathways to access youth in addition to during the school day—all designed to promote positive youth development within this community. This required a communitywide effort through collaboration with working linkages to the university campus. The first step in this process, the adaptation of a youth survey provided by the extension specialist on campus, took almost two years of working together with the community. Although this may seem like a long time, this was a critical aspect of developing a strong collaboration with the university and multiple community organizations to establish high levels of leadership, trust, and productivity; equally shared ideas and decisions; and structured formal and informal communication.[7] The high school and middle school administrators, counselors, and teachers; parents; youth; and community organizations such as Youth Count, Children's Council, Teen Pregnancy Prevention Program, Youth Leadership Student Council, Character Education, and the Tobacco Prevention Program—County Health Department;

social services; law enforcement; and the judicial system were all involved.

Local data on ethical thoughts and behaviors

In November 2003, high school youth in grades 9 through 12 completed the 136-item survey. A total of 1,285 (96 percent) surveys were included in analyses. Forty-six percent of respondents were female, and 54 percent were male.

Six questions asked youth about how they perceived themselves in terms of specific thoughts and actions concerning right and wrong. Consistent with previous research, results indicate that surveyed youth characterized themselves as thinking more than acting in ethical ways:

- 80 percent "strongly agreed" or "agreed" that it is not worth it to lie or cheat because it hurts your character.
- 87 percent "strongly agreed" or "agreed" that it is important to be kind, caring, and compassionate.
- 88 percent "strongly agreed" or "agreed" that it is important to them to be a person with good character.
- 72 percent reported that they treated others with respect, even if they were different from them, "always" or "a lot of the time."
- 60 percent indicated that they deal peacefully with anger, insults, and disagreements "always" or "a lot of the time."
- 59 percent said that they think before they act and considered the consequences of their choices "always" or "a lot of the time."

To see if our data exhibited a distinction between thoughts and actions as seen in previous studies, we submitted the six character questions to factor analysis. Results of the factor analysis provided two main components that appeared to confirm the distinction between thoughts and actions. The mean score for Thoughts was 2.27, indicating that participants' thoughts about character were quite positive overall. The mean score for Actions was 3.49; this slightly higher mean shows that participants' actions were slightly less positive than their thoughts.

A cross-tabulation of Thoughts by Actions scores produced interesting results. Of the 1,194 students, only 89 students (7 percent) indicated that they are consistently positive in how they think and how they act regarding right and wrong. Conversely, only 18 (2 percent) students indicated that they never act in accordance with what they consider ethical behavior. That leaves the vast majority (1,087, or 91 percent) of students with some contradiction between what they believe and how they act.

As a specific example of this discrepancy between thoughts and actions, we looked at only those students who agreed or strongly agreed with the statement, "It's not worth it to lie or cheat because it hurts my character." When we examined their responses to the question, "In the last six months, how often have you cheated on a class test?" we found that 54 percent responded "never" and 46 percent responded "at least once." This is an apparent mismatch between stated thoughts about cheating and actions. These local data give additional credibility to previous findings.

─────────────

Local data on out-of-school time

The question now becomes: Other than school, where and when can the community access young people to give them opportunities to discuss, experience, make mistakes, and have success in developing an understanding of their own ethics? What pathways might exist or be created that will create opportunities to bring thoughts and actions into agreement?

To answer this question, we turned to the survey data on out-of-school-time use. The responses indicated that 69 percent of these high school youth never spend time in nonschool clubs or organizations such as 4-H, Girl or Boy Scouts, Boys and Girls Clubs, or other youth groups. Yet at least once a week:

• 76 percent participate in out-of-school activities or hobbies such as music or dance lessons, hiking, biking, or reading.

- 60 percent participate in extracurricular activities such as sports, yearbook, or pep club.
- 47 percent are involved in religious activities.

Then we looked at the overlap among out-of-school, extracurricular, and religious activities. We found that only 12 percent of the students report that they do none of these types of activities, 25 percent do one, 34 percent do two, and 30 percent do all three types of activities. Clearly, there are three out-of-school pathways to more than 88 percent of the youth in this particular high school population.

The collaboration felt it was important to ask all youth about opportunities for leadership and decision making in out-of-school-time activities. Two questions on this topic were included in the survey. The first asked about the extent to which young people are involved as equal partners with adults, and the second asked about the extent to which young people participate in planning and decision making. While 39 percent of the youth reported teens "never" or "rarely" work as equal partners with adults, 42 percent reported "sometimes" or "about half the time," and 19 percent reported "most of the time" or "always." Similarly, 39 percent reported that young people participate in planning and decision making "never" or "rarely," 44 percent reported "sometimes" or "about half the time," and 18 percent reported "most of the time" or "always."

In summary, more than half the youth respondents believe that in their out-of-school-time activities, teens have opportunities to be equal partners with adults and participate in planning and decision making at least sometimes, consistent with the mutuality in teaching, learning, and action described by Zeldin, McDaniel, Topitzes, and Lorens.[8] As we consider the situational or contextual influences on the development of ethics, these are important factors to consider.

***

Action planning

We now have local information on where and when to access young people, in addition to some basic information about how teens interact with adults during out-of-school activities. What is the community doing with this and other information gleaned from the youth survey to promote character and positive youth development?

After some time to read the report that presented the survey findings in the context of what we know about adolescent development and risk and resilience, the community collaboration committee planned a full-day work session with its university partner. The purpose was to try to absorb the overwhelming amount of data and develop a three-year strategic community action plan. Strategic actions or priorities were identified in several areas: teen health and well-being, school and community, substance use, family, and activities and delinquency.

Action teams were formed with specific strategic directions, tasks, target audience, leadership, and time lines established. Community-university action teams identified research-based program models for implementation and developed evaluation plans to measure program effectiveness. Currently this community is in the early stages of the process of program development and implementation.

Lessons learned

The greatest benefit to the community, for both adults and youth, is the strong local investment generated by the process of building a collaboration to hear the youth voice, adapting the survey, collecting the data, digesting the results, and working together to respond to expressed needs and build on strengths. No longer could parents, teachers, elected officials, and other stakeholders say, "It's not like that in our community." The community-university partnership has been operating with sustained membership for six years and has empowered residents as experts in local youth issues. The process of creating working partnerships between communities and universities, especially with cooperative extension, can be replicated anywhere.

Concerning our understanding of ethics in youth, there are several lessons:

The vast majority of high school students, nationally and in this community, think of themselves as more ethical than their behavior indicates. Recognition and acceptance of this fact will help adults engage youth in meaningful experiences and discussions.

Understanding when and where we can access youth during out-of-school time can help us be strategic in planning and using resources.

Emphasis on positive youth development, including character education, is crucial to the success of out-of-school, extracurricular, and religious activities.

Training of adult youth workers and volunteers must include information on the development of ethics, including the differences between thoughts, feelings, and actions about right and wrong.

Training of adults must also include ways to work with youth as partners with more than token involvement in planning and decision making.

Research is needed to develop a scale of ethical development in youth that includes all three factors: thoughts, feelings, and actions. This community addressed only thoughts and actions.

Perhaps Lickona stated it most clearly: "As people grow in their character they will develop an increasingly refined understanding of the core values, a deeper commitment to living according to those values and a stronger tendency to behave in accordance with those values."[9] The job of communities is to provide the opportunities for young people to develop the skills and competencies during out-of-school time that will serve them well as they gain greater understanding of their own ethics. We want young people who can be empathetic to others, understand the situation, and guide their own behavior in accordance with what they believe is right.

Notes

1. Howard, R. W., Berkowitz, M. W., & Schaeffer, E. F. (2004). Politics of character education. *Educational Policy, 18,* 188–215.

2. Lickona, T. (1989). *Educating for character: How our schools can teach respect and responsibility.* New York: Bantam.

3. The Character Education Partnership (n.d.). *The eleven principles.* Retrieved November 4, 2005, from http://www.character.org/site/c.gwKU-JhNYJrF/b.993263/k.72EC/The_Eleven_Principles.htm.

4. Lickona, T. (1996). Eleven principles of effective character education. *Journal of Moral Education, 25*, 93–100.

5. Howard, et al. (2004).

6. U.S. Census Bureau. Census 2000, Summary File 1 (SF 1) and Summary File 3 (SF 3), generated by James Roebuck using American Factfinder. Retrieved July 25, 2005, http://factfinder.census.gov/.

7. Borden, L. M., Hogue, T., & Perkins, D. F. (1998). *Community collaborations: A guide to the standards of practice supporting youth and families.* Columbus, OH: National Network for Collaboration.

8. Zeldin, S., McDaniel, A., Topitzes, D., & Lorens, M. B. (2001). Bringing young people to the table: Effects on adults and youth organizations. *CYF Journal, 2*(2), 20–27.

9. Lickona. (1996). P. 94.

DONNA J. PETERSON *is an associate research scientist in the John and Doris Norton School of Family and Consumer Sciences at the University of Arizona.*

JAMES C. ROEBUCK *is a research specialist in the John and Doris Norton School of Family and Consumer Sciences at the University of Arizona.*

SHERRY C. BETTS *is a professor and extension specialist in the John and Doris Norton School of Family and Consumer Sciences at the University of Arizona.*

MARTA E. STUART *is an associate agent in cooperative extension at the University of Arizona.*

Index

145

Notes for Contributors

New Directions for Youth Development: Theory, Practice, and Research is a quarterly publication focusing on contemporary issues challenging the field of youth development. A defining focus of the journal is the relationship among theory, research, and practice. In particular, *NDYD* is dedicated to recognizing resilience as well as risk, and healthy development of our youth as well as the difficulties of adolescence. The journal is intended as a forum for provocative discussion that reaches across the worlds of academia, service, philanthropy, and policy.

In the tradition of the New Directions series, each volume of the journal addresses a single, timely topic, although special issues covering a variety of topics are occasionally commissioned. We welcome submissions of both volume topics and individual articles. All articles should specifically address the implications of theory for practice and research directions, and how these arenas can better inform one another. Articles may focus on any aspect of youth development; all theoretical and methodological orientations are welcome.

If you would like to be an *issue editor*, please submit an outline of no more than four pages that includes a brief description of your proposed topic and its significance along with a brief synopsis of individual articles (including tentative authors and a working title for each chapter).

If you would like to be an *author*, please submit first a draft of an abstract of no more than 1,500 words, including a two-sentence synopsis of the article; send this to the editorial assistant.

For all prospective issue editors or authors:

- Please make sure to keep accessibility in mind, by illustrating theoretical ideas with specific examples and explaining technical terms in nontechnical language. A busy practitioner who may not have an extensive research background should be well served by our work.

- Please keep in mind that references should be limited to twenty-five to thirty. Authors should make use of case examples to illustrate their ideas, rather than citing exhaustive research references. You may want to recommend two or three key articles, books, or Web sites that are influential in the field, to be featured on a resource page. This can be used by readers who want to delve more deeply into a particular topic.
- All reference information should be listed as endnotes, rather than including author names in the body of the article or footnotes at the bottom of the page. The endnotes are in APA style.

Please visit http://www.pearweb.org for more information.

Gil G. Noam
Editor-in-Chief

Back Issue/Subscription Order Form

Copy or detach and send to:

Jossey-Bass, A Wiley Imprint, 989 Market Street, San Francisco, CA 94103-1741

Call or fax toll-free: Phone 888-378-2537 6:30AM – 3PM PST; Fax 888-481-2665

Back Issues: Please send me the following issues at $29 each

(Important: please include series initials and issue number, such as YD100.)

_____

_____

_____

$ _____ Total for single issues

$ _____

SHIPPING CHARGES: SURFACE	Domestic	Canadian
First Item	$5.00	$6.00
Each Add'l Item	$3.00	$1.50

For next-day and second-day delivery rates, call the number listed above.

Subscriptions: Please __start __renew my subscription to _New Directions for Youth Development_ for the year 2____ at the following rate:

U.S.	__Individual $80	__Institutional $180
Canada	__Individual $80	__Institutional $220
All Others	__Individual $104	__Institutional $254

For more information about online subscriptions visit
www.interscience.wiley.com

$ _____ Total single issues and subscriptions (Add appropriate sales tax for your state for single issue orders. No sales tax for U.S. subscriptions. Canadian residents, add GST for subscriptions and single issues.)

__Payment enclosed (U.S. check or money order only)

__VISA __MC __AmEx #_____ Exp. Date _____

Signature _____ Day Phone _____

__ Bill Me (U.S. institutional orders only. Purchase order required.)

Purchase order # _____

Federal Tax ID13559302   **GST 89102 8052**

Name _____

Address _____

_____

Phone _____ E-mail _____

For more information about Jossey-Bass, visit our Web site at **www.josseybass.com**

Other Titles Available

YD105 **Participation in Youth Programs: Enrollment, Attendance, and Engagement**
Heather B. Weiss, Priscilla M. D. Little, Suzanne M. Bouffard, Editors
This timely volume proposes that to understand and intervene to improve participation in out-of-school time (OST) programs, issues of access, enrollment, and engagement must be considered, and in the context of program quality. Contributing authors pose a three-part equation where participation = enrollment + attendance + engagement, and examine these three critical components of overall participation in out-of-school time programs. Chapters provide research-based strategies on how to increase participation, and how to define, measure, and study it, drawing from the latest developmental research and evaluation literature.
ISBN: 0-7879-8053-6

YD104 **Professional Development for Youth Workers**
Pam Garza, Lynne M. Borden, Kirk A. Astroth
Professional development of caring, capable adults who interact with and on behalf of youth is a key issue for youth organizations and agencies committed to creating environments that nurture young people's growth and transition into adulthood. This issue offers a glimpse of some of the innovated, sustained, and coordinated efforts to advance the preparation and support of youth workers based on the principles of positive youth development. Contributors provide examples demonstrating how to support youth work interaction as well as training networks that take common approaches to professional development and outline some of the significant challenges faced in youth worker professional development and their solutions. From defining competencies for entry-level youth workers to case studies that explore the role of colleges and universities in professionalizing the field, this issue serves as a record of the evolution of the youth development field and a call for its continued progress in building a comprehensive system that can meet the needs of both youth workers and the young people they come into contact with each day.
ISBN 0-7879-7861-2

YD103 **The Transforming Power of Adult-Youth Relationships**
Gil G. Noam, Nina Fiore
Introducing various perspectives that look at the changes in theories, attitudes, approaches, and practices in adult-youth relationships, this issue stresses a model of growth based on partnership and connection over older theories of autonomy and hierarchy between adults and youth. These ways of viewing young people's contributions as extremely important to societal development have to be increasingly embedded in a perspective that young people grow and thrive in relationships and that social institutions, especially families, schools, and youth-serving organizations, have to

change dramatically. Contributors also demonstrate how much common ground exists between older and emerging models of youth development and how much work remains to be done.
ISBN 0-7879-7788-8

YD102   **Negotiation: Interpersonal Approaches to Intergroup Conflict**
Daniel L. Shapiro, Brooke E. Clayton
This issue considers the emotional complexities of intergroup conflict. The chapter authors examine the relational challenges that youth encounter in dealing with conflict and, combining innovative theory with ambitious practical application, identify conflict management strategies. These interventions have affected millions of youth across the continents.
ISBN 0-7879-7649-0

YD101   **After-School Worlds: Creating a New Social Space for Development and Learning**
Gil G. Noam
Showcases a variety of large-scale policy initiatives, effective institutional collaborations, and innovative programming options that produce high-quality environments in which young people are realizing their potential. Contributors underscore the conditions—from fostering interagency partnerships, to structuring organized out-of-school-time activities, to encouraging staff-student relationships—that lay the groundwork for positive youth development after school. At the same time, their examples illuminate the challenges for policymakers, researchers, and educators to redefine the field of afterschool as a whole, including the search for a shared lexicon, the push to preserve the character of afterschool as an intermediary space, and the need to create and further programs that are grounded in reliable research and that demonstrate success.
ISBN 0-7879-7304-1

YD100   **Understanding the Social Worlds of Immigrant Youth**
Carola Suárez-Orozco, Irina L. G. Todorova
This issue seeks to deepen understanding of the major social influences that shape immigrant youths' paths in their transition to the United States. The authors delve into a number of social worlds that can contribute to the positive development of immigrant youth. They also provide insight into sources of information about identity pathway options available to those youth. The chapters offer new data regarding the developmental opportunities that family roles and responsibilities, school contexts, community organizations, religious involvement and beliefs, gendered expectations, and media influences present.
ISBN 0-7879-7267-3

adolescence as well as institutional barriers to youth involvement, the efforts of these organizations engaged in youth participation programs deserve careful analysis and support. This volume offers an assessment of the field, as well as specific chapters that chronicle efforts to achieve youth participation across a variety of settings and dimensions.
ISBN 0-7879-6339-9

YD95   **Pathways to Positive Development Among Diverse Youth**
Richard M. Lerner, Carl S. Taylor, Alexander von Eye
Positive youth development represents an emerging emphasis in developmental thinking that is focused on the incredible potential of adolescents to maintain healthy trajectories and develop resilience, even in the face of myriad negative influences. This volume discusses the theory, research, policy, and programs that take this strength-based, positive development approach to diverse youth. It examines theoretical ideas about the nature of positive youth development, and about the related concepts of thriving and well-being, as well as current and needed policy strategies, "best practice" in youth-serving programs, and promising community-based efforts to marshal the developmental assets of individuals and communities to enhance thriving among youth.
ISBN 0-7879-6338-0

YD94   **Youth Development and After-School Time: A Tale of Many Cities**
Gil G. Noam, Beth Miller
This issue looks at exciting citywide and cross-city initiatives in after-school time. It presents case studies of youth-related work that combines large-scale policy, developmental thinking, and innovative programming, as well as research and evaluation. Chapters discuss efforts of community-based organizations, museums, universities, schools, and clinics who are joining forces, sharing funding and other resources, and jointly creating a system of after-school care and education.
ISBN 0-7879-6337-2

YD93   **A Critical View of Youth Mentoring**
Jean E. Rhodes
Mentoring has become an almost essential aspect of youth development and is expanding beyond the traditional one-to-one, volunteer, community-based mentoring. This volume provides evidence of the benefits of enduring high-quality mentoring programs, as well as apprenticeships, advisories, and other relationship-based programs that show considerable promise. Authors examine mentoring in the workplace, teacher-student interaction, and the mentoring potential of student advising programs. They also take a critical look at the importance of youth-adult relationships and how a deeper understanding of these relationships can benefit youth mentoring.

This issue raises important questions about relationship-based interventions and generates new perspectives on the role of adults in the lives of youth.
ISBN 0-7879-6294-5

YD92   **Zero Tolerance: Can Suspension and Expulsion Keep Schools Safe?**
Russell J. Skiba, Gil G. Noam
Addressing the problem of school violence and disruption requires thoughtful understanding of the complexity of the personal and systemic factors that increase the probability of violence, and designing interventions based on that understanding. This inaugural issue explores the effectiveness of zero tolerance as a tool for promoting school safety and improving student behavior and offers alternative strategies that work.
ISBN 0-7879-1441-X

NEW DIRECTIONS FOR YOUTH DEVELOPMENT
IS NOW AVAILABLE ONLINE AT WILEY INTERSCIENCE

What is Wiley InterScience?

Wiley InterScience is the dynamic online content service from John Wiley & Sons delivering the full text of over 300 leading scientific, technical, medical, and professional journals, plus major reference works, the acclaimed *Current Protocols* laboratory manuals, and even the full text of select Wiley print books online.

What are some special features of Wiley InterScience?

Wiley InterScience Alerts is a service that delivers table of contents via e-mail for any journal available on Wiley InterScience as soon as a new issue is published online.

Early View is Wiley's exclusive service presenting individual articles online as soon as they are ready, even before the release of the compiled print issue. These articles are complete, peer-reviewed, and citable.

CrossRef is the innovative multi-publisher reference linking system enabling readers to move seamlessly from a reference in a journal article to the cited publication, typically located on a different server and published by a different publisher.

How can I access Wiley InterScience?

Visit http://www.interscience.wiley.com

Guest Users can browse Wiley InterScience for unrestricted access to journal Tables of Contents and Article Abstracts, or use the powerful search engine.

Registered Users are provided with a *Personal Home Page* to store and manage customized alerts, searches, and links to favorite journals and articles. Additionally, Registered Users can view free Online Sample Issues and preview selected material from major reference works.

Licensed Customers are entitled to access full-text journal articles in PDF, with select journals also offering full-text HTML.

How do I become an Authorized User?

Authorized Users are individuals authorized by a paying Customer to have access to the journals in Wiley InterScience. For example, a university that subscribes to Wiley journals is considered to be the Customer. Faculty, staff, and students authorized by the university to have access to those journals in Wiley InterScience are Authorized Users. Users should contact their Library for information on which Wiley journals they have access to in Wiley InterScience.

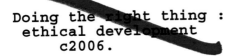